52

VOLUME **ONE**

GEOFF **JOHNS**

GRANT **MORRISON**

GREG **RUCKA**

MARK **WAID**

52 VOLUME **ONE**

Dan DiDio Senior VP-Executive Editor **Stephen Wacker** Editor-original series **Jann Jones Harvey Richards** Assistant Editors-original series **Anton Kawasaki** Editor-collected edition **Robbin Brosterman** Senior Art Director **Paul Levitz** President & Publisher **Georg Brewer** VP-Design & DC Direct Creative **Richard Bruning** Senior VP-Creative Director **Patrick Caldon** Executive VP-Finance & Operations **Chris Caramalis** VP-Finance **John Cunningham** VP-Marketing **Terri Cunningham** VP-Managing Editor **Alison Gill** VP-Manufacturing **Hank Kanalz** VP-General Manager, WildStorm **Jim Lee** Editorial Director-WildStorm **Paula Lowitt** Senior VP-Business & Legal Affairs **MaryEllen McLaughlin** VP-Advertising & Custom Publishing **John Nee** VP-Business Development **Gregory Noveck** Senior VP-Creative Affairs **Sue Pohja** VP-Book Trade Sales **Cheryl Rubin** Senior VP-Brand Management **Jeff Trojan** VP-Business Development, DC Direct **Bob Wayne** VP-Sales

Special thanks to Joe Prado on Week Two and Ivan Cohen on Week Ten
Cover by J.G. Jones with Alex Sinclair
Publication design by Robbie Biederman

52: Volume One

DC Comics, 1700 Broadway, New York, NY 10019. A Warner Bros. Entertainment Company. Printed in Canada. First Printing.
ISBN: 1-4012-1353-7 ISBN 13: 978-1-4012-1353-4

art breakdowns **KEITH GIFFEN** pencils **EDDY BARROWS, CHRIS BATISTA, JOE BENNETT, KEN LASHLEY, SHAWN MOLL, TODD NAUCK**

inks **MARLO ALQUIZA, DRAXHALL, JACK JADSON, RUY JOSÉ, TOM NGUYEN, JIMMY PALMIOTTI, ROB STULL** colors **DAVID BARON, ALEX SINCLAIR** letters **PHIL BALSMAN, PAT BROSSEAU, JARED K. FLETCHER, TRAVIS LANHAM, ROB LEIGH, NICK J. NAPOLITANO**

original covers **J.G. JONES** with **ALEX SINCLAIR**

PREVIOUSLY . . .

Maxwell Lord, the "Black King" of the government agency known as Checkmate, had been secretly gathering sensitive information on the world's super-heroes with the help of Brother Eye — a machine originally built by BATMAN, but now taken over by Lord for sinister purposes. Using his mental powers, Lord was able to take control of the mind of the world's most powerful hero, SUPERMAN, and used the Man of Steel to beat up Batman and attack WONDER WOMAN. The Amazing Amazon eventually bound Lord in her "lasso of truth," forcing him to tell her how to stop the rampaging Superman from potentially causing countless deaths and massive destruction. Lord replied with the only solution available: "Kill me."

Seeing no other choice, Wonder Woman snapped Lord's neck, freeing Superman. But neither the Man of Steel nor the Dark Knight could condone Wonder Woman's actions — believing that there could have been another way to stop Lord.

Soon after, a CRISIS of infinite proportions was rocking the DC Universe to its core, and the Teen Titan known as Superboy sacrificed his life in order to save Earth. Meanwhile, *another* Superboy from an alternate dimension (Earth-Prime) attempted to change *this* Earth into a simpler, less-violent world — but, in doing so, became more violent himself. Superman and other heroes stopped the rampaging Superboy-Prime by flying him through Krypton's red sun, Rao. Superboy-Prime was stopped, but as a result Superman lost all of his powers. The hero ultimately retired his cape, choosing to focus on his life as reporter Clark Kent and husband to Lois Lane.

Batman, realizing he had become too paranoid in his war on crime, decided to leave Gotham for a year and retrace his steps toward becoming Batman — taking Tim Drake (Robin) and Dick Grayson (Nightwing) along with him. Wonder Woman also took a year off from her duties to do some soul-searching of her own.

The Crisis was over, and through all the chaos a "new Earth" was born — a world without its three greatest champions: Superman, Batman and Wonder Woman.

But it was *not* a world without heroes...

Week 1, Day 1

RALPH, YOU'RE BREAKING UP.
THAT OBVIOUS?
ANSELMO CASE 1995

YEAH, RECEPTION STINKS EVERYWHERE TODAY.
AH. NOT QUITE WHAT I'M--
BUT IT'S GREAT TO HEAR YOUR VOICE, BECAUSE GREEN LANTERN HEARD THE SECRET SOCIETY TORE PRETTY HARD THROUGH OPAL CITY. THEY DO MUCH DAMAGE?
HOME OF THE JUSTICE LEAGUE'S WORLD-FAMOUS ELONGATED MAN DUCTILE DETECTIVE
RALPH?
RALPH, WHAT HAPPENED?

--HEROES, SUPER-VILLAINS, THROW IN THE WRATH OF GOD COMING DOWN--
NO, MAN, I'M A GOTHAMITE BORN AND BRED, I'VE SEEN IT ALL, RIGHT?
EARTHQUAKES, PLAGUES AND POISON IN THE RESERVOIR, AND I SWEAR I THOUGHT IT WAS THE END OF THE WORLD LAST NIGHT.

IT WAS.
WHAT, YOU FIND YOURSELF WITH AN EMPTY BOTTLE, MONTOYA?
FUNNY GUY. KEEP 'EM COMING.
YOU HEARD ABOUT BLÜDHAVEN, RIGHT? MY SISTER HAD FAMILY THERE, THEY SAY SUPERMAN...

WHO LIVED THROUGH THIS?

WE ARE NOT YET CERTAIN, MONSIEUR STEEL, BUT WE ARE GRATEFUL FOR THE SEARCH ASSIST.
THIS WAS MY SON'S SCHOOL.
I HAVE NOT SEEN HIM SINCE MONDAY.

Week 1, Day 2

...THEY SAY THE JSA AND THE TITANS ARE DIGGING OUT THE EAST COAST, RALPH...
...IN THE MEANTIME, RUMOR IS FLYING AROUND MUCH MORE QUICKLY THAN ACTUAL IN-FORMATION.
NO ONE'S SEEN FLASH AT ALL. BATGIRL WAS REPORTED IN HOUSTON AND IN TORONTO AND, ACTUALLY, PROBABLY NEITHER.
BUT YOU HAVE HEARD WHO FOR SURE DIDN'T MAKE IT OUT ALIVE, RIGHT?
SUPERBOY.

THAT'S A CRYING SHAME, YOU ASK ME. JUST A KID, TOO. SAVED MY BROTHER FROM THE JOKER ONCE--
YOU, UH... YOU MIGHT WANT TO SLOW DOWN THERE, MONTOYA.
...OR YOU COULD POUR FASTER.
KNIGHTS

NEED A DOCTOR OVER HERE!
GIVE ME THE BULLET.
MULTIPLE BURNS, LEFT LEG HAS A TIB-FIB FRACTURE. SAID SOMEONE WITH A BOW SAVED HIM FROM AN OMAC UNIT, THEN MAY HAVE GOTTEN DUSTED.
HAS ANYONE HERE SEEN GREEN ARROW?

Week 1, Day 3
HE IS? FINALLY, SOME GOOD NEWS.
BUT WE STILL DON'T KNOW ABOUT ADAM STRANGE, RIGHT?
SUE ALWAYS LIKED HIM.
NO, BEA, THERE WASN'T MUCH LEFT OF HER-- OUR-- STUFF.
MOSTLY SOME OF THE WEIRDER CASE SOUVENIRS. PRETTY MUCH...
...PRETTY MUCH ALL I HAVE LEFT.
I...
...I HAVE TO GO NOW, BEA.
...TO THE MEMORIAL SERVICE LATER THIS WEEK IN METROPOLIS FOR EVERYONE WHO DIED.

IF THE ROADS ARE OPEN, YOU... YOU WANNA, Y'KNOW, GO?
NO, THANKS...
Cannon Cigarett

...HAD MY SHARE OF FUNERALS LATELY...
52

Week 1, Day 4

...SO THE SHORT OF IT IS, AFTER YEARS AND YEARS OF HITTING AND RUNNING, ALL THE SUPER-VILLAINS... AND I MEAN ALL OF THEM... TEAMED UP. DECLARED ALL-OUT WAR ON THE WHITE HATS.

PICKED US OFF IN TWOS AND THREES BEFORE MOUNTING AN ATTACK THE LIKES OF WHICH SHOULD, BY ALL RIGHTS, HAVE RIPPED THIS PLANET IN HALF.

SO, BASICALLY, WE JUST CAME BACK FROM THE BRINK OF ANNIHILATION.

YOU KNOW, WHEN YOU PUT IT LIKE THAT, NO WONDER WE'RE PRETTY MUCH EXHAUSTED.

BUT THE DANGER'S PASSED. THE GOOD GUYS WON THEIR BIGGEST FIGHT EVER.

YEP.

AND WE'RE SAFE AGAIN.

RELATIVELY SPEAKING.

OKAY. SO...

...WHEN DO THINGS GO BACK TO NORMAL?

Week 1, Day 5

LOOK! UP IN THE SKY!

Siegel St.

Shuster Rd.

HOT DIDIDOGS

Metropolis Taxi

FLEISCHER BROS. TRANS

BOOSTER GOLD, LADIES AND GENTLEMEN!
HE'S FROM THE FUTURE!
HOW COOL IS THAT?
LIT BEER
AND EVEN THOUGH BOOSTER'S WAY TOO MODEST TO SAY IT, I'M NOT ASHAMED TO SPEAK UP AND TELL YOU THIS MAN IS THE FRESH NEW FACE OF SUPER-HEROICS.
WHAT THE %@&% IS ALL THIS, YA FLAMIN' GALA? HUH?
PICKING ON ME?
I DIDN'T EVEN KNOW I WAS GONNA NICK THOSE DIAMONDS 'TIL I DID IT! SPUR O' THE MOMENT! HOW'D YA GET UP ON ME SO QUICK?
CALL IT AN INSIDE TIP, MAMMOTH.
BOYS, GIRLS, AND CORPORATE SPONSORS-- IF THE DAY NEEDS SAVING, BOOSTER'S YOUR GUY!
IN AN UNCERTAIN WORLD, IT'S GOOD TO KNOW THERE ARE STILL SOME THINGS YOU CAN ALWAYS RELY ON.

BAM

SIR--
I SEE IT, SKEETS.
PHOTO-OP *DELUXE.*

HEY THERE, LITTLE LADY.
WHAT'S UP?
MY BROTHER SAID *WONDER WOMAN* WAS DEAD.
HE SAID SHE WAS *GONE* AND SHE'S NEVER COMING BACK.

IS THAT RIGHT?
WELL, I'VE SEEN THE FUTURE AND HAPPEN TO KNOW WONDER WOMAN'S FINE. THEY'RE *ALL* FINE.
NOW STEP ASIDE, KIDS.

TERRIFIC TAKEDOWN, SIR.
YOU'RE A REAL PRO.
THANK MAMMOTH HERE, SKEETS.
HE'S THE ONE WHO KEPT IT FROM BEING A DULL AFTERNOON.
GROAAAN

DC COMICS 52

NOTHING TO SEE HERE, FOLKS.
JUST DOING MY JOB.
NOW, IF YOU'LL EXCUSE ME...

WRITTEN BY GEOFF JOHNS, GRANT MORRISON, GREG RUCKA, MARK WAI

ART BREAKDOWNS BY KEITH GIFFEN • PENCILS BY JOE BENNETT • INKS BY RUY JOS
COLORS BY ALEX SINCLAIR • LETTERING BY NICK J. NAPOLITANO

ASSISTANT EDITORS JANN JONES & HARVEY RICHARDS EDITED BY STEPHEN WACKER
COVER BY J.G. JONES & ALEX SINCLAIR

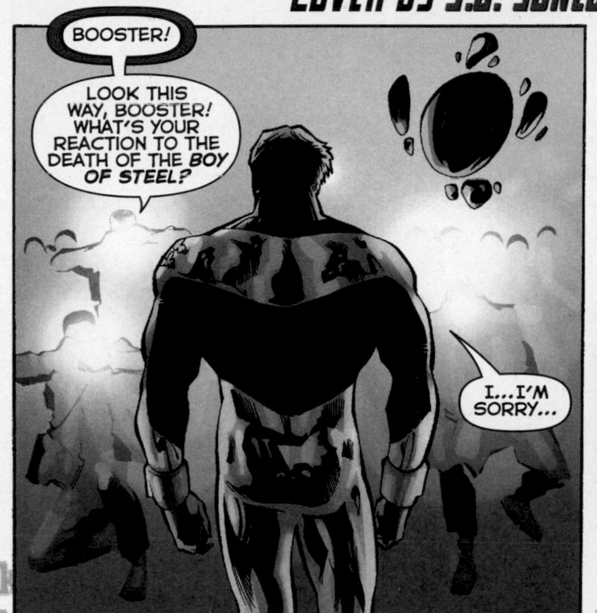

GOLDEN LADS & LASSES MUST...

YOU KNOW, TECHNICALLY, SIR, I'M THE ONE HOLDING ALL THE HISTORICAL DATA FROM THIS ERA.
I CAN'T EVEN GET YOU TO READ THE FILES...
AND THAT IS WHY WE MAKE SUCH A GREAT TEAM.
A COUPLE OF REFUGEES FROM THE 25TH CENTURY COME BACK TO THE HEROIC AGE ARMED ONLY WITH FUTURE WEAPONRY, CHARM, AND EVERY NEWS HEADLINE FOR THE NEXT HALF MILLENNIUM.

I WISH I COULD'VE TOLD THAT LITTLE GIRL BACK THERE WHAT TOMORROW IS. MY BIG DAY.
I MAY HAVE FLUNKED TWENTY-FIRST CENTURY HISTORY--
AMONG YOUR MANY ACCOMPLISH-MENTS, SIR.
--BUT EVEN I KNOW THAT TOMORROW IS THE DEFINING MOMENT OF THE CENTURY AND I'M GONNA BE PART OF IT.

THE SPEECH OF HOPE AND UNITY THAT SUPERMAN DELIVERS WILL BE TAUGHT IN CIVICS CLASSES FOR THE NEXT FIVE HUNDRED YEARS.
AND THAT PHOTO OF HIM, BATMAN AND WONDER WOMAN AS THEY ANNOUNCE THE NEW JUSTICE LEAGUE? FAMOUS. OLSEN GETS A HOWITZER FOR IT.
PULITZER, SIR.

WHATEVER. THE DAWN OF THIS CENTURY'S JLA. AND THEY'RE GOING TO ASK ME TO JOIN, AREN'T THEY? C'MON. YOU CAN TELL ME.
I ALREADY HAVE, SIR.
SO TELL ME AGAIN. MAKE ME SMILE.
SKEETS, BEING A MEMBER OF THE GREATEST JUSTICE LEAGUE EVER--

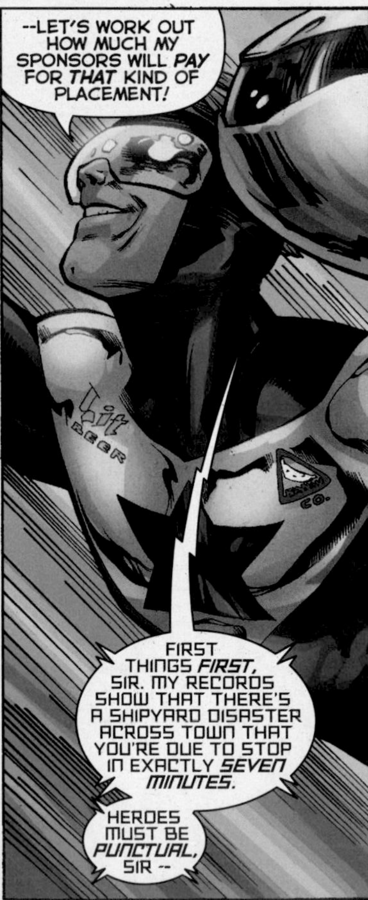
--LET'S WORK OUT HOW MUCH MY SPONSORS WILL PAY FOR THAT KIND OF PLACEMENT!
FIRST THINGS FIRST, SIR. MY RECORDS SHOW THAT THERE'S A SHIPYARD DISASTER ACROSS TOWN THAT YOU'RE DUE TO STOP IN EXACTLY SEVEN MINUTES.
HEROES MUST BE PUNCTUAL, SIR --

--IF NOTHING ELSE.
MY BEER
Soder Cola

AMBASSADOR HOT
YOU HAVE TWO VOICEMAIL MESSAGES.
MESSAGE ONE:

RALPH, IT'S BEA. CALL ME WHEN YOU GET THIS, OKAY? I WORRY ABOUT YOU.
OBITUARIES
SUSAN DEARBON DIBNY
AMBASSADOR HOTEL
I KNOW YOU'VE KIND OF MADE A POINT OF AVOIDING SORTING THROUGH THE HOUSE SINCE SUE DIED, AND NOW YOU DON'T HAVE ANY CHOICE, AND...

...WELL, THAT HAS TO BE TOUGH. THE MEMORIAL'S TOMORROW... WHICH IS GOOD, BECAUSE I DON'T IMAGINE WE'LL HAVE A DEFINITIVE ROLL CALL OF WHO'S STILL AROUND UNTIL WE'RE ALL IN ONE PLACE... BUT WE ALL WANT TO SEE YOU. COME BY, OKAY?
WE MISS HER, TOO, RALPH.

WE MISS HER, TOO.

BEEP
MESSAGE TWO:

MR. DIBNY, THIS IS ELYSIUM MORTUARY? WE'RE THE ONES WHO HANDLED YOUR WIFE'S FUNERAL ARRANGEMENTS?

SIR, WE... WE DON'T KNOW HOW TO TELL YOU THIS, BUT... THE CEMETERY CALLED, AND THEY SAY THEY FOUND A... A MESSAGE...

...ON MRS. DIBNY'S TOMBSTONE.

DAILY PLANET

NATASHA! SET IT DOWN, YOUNG LADY!

UNCLE JOHN--

NOW!

NO, IT'S THE ARMOR I GAVE TO YOU...

BA-DIP
...AND IT'S CLEAR TO ME YOU HAVEN'T EARNED IT.

HEY! WHAT--
--WHAT'D YOU DO? IT'S LOCKING UP!
DA
DA
DEEP

NO!
WHAT ARE YOU DOING?!?

THERE ARE PEOPLE OUT THERE DOING MORE WITH FAR LESS, NAT.
YOU WANT ARMOR? BUILD IT YOURSELF.

YOU CAN START WORK ON IT WHEN YOU GET HOME.

<IN MY ATTEMPT TO PROTECT OUR HOMELAND, I TURNED MY BACK ON THE REST OF THE WORLD.
<AND I SUFFERED FOR IT.>
<I WITNESSED THE TRUE EVIL THAT LIVES WITHIN SO MANY AND I REALIZED THAT KAHNDAQ MUST TEACH THE WORLD HOW TO DEAL WITH IT.>
<WE HAVE A MISSION.>
<I WILL BE YOUR AMBASSADOR OF JUSTICE.>
<I WILL LEAD THE WORLD BY EXAMPLE.>
THEMYSCIRA HOUSE
<AND I WILL SPREAD OUR NEW GOSPEL.>
EMBASSY OF KAHNDAQ
<MAY THE GODS BE WITH US-->
<-- BECAUSE THEY WILL NOT STAND A CHANCE AGAINST US.>
<YOU ARE NO MESSENGER, BLACK ADAM!>

‹YOU AND ALL OF KAHNDAQ ARE HERETICS POWERED BY LIES!
‹MY PEOPLE REFUSE YOUR WIS--!›
--DOM!?
AAAAARRR!
KRRKKRIPP
‹YOU HAVE THREE MORE CHANCES TO TELL ME WHO SENT YOU.›

Week 1, Day 6
OH...THIS IS NO FUN TO WATCH.
WHERE'S CAPTAIN MARVEL?
...GATHERING SINCE EARLY THIS MORNING IN METROPOLIS. THOUSANDS ARE EXPECTED TO SHOW UP FOR TODAY'S EVENT...
BLACK ADAM IS MUCH TOO SERIOUS FOR ME.
AND NOW HE THINKS HE CAN "CHANGE" THE WORLD?
HA!
MAGIC DOESN'T CHANGE THE WORLD!
SCIENCE DOES.
SCIENCE BEATS MAGIC!
CNN LIVE
ISN'T THAT RIGHT, MY LITTLE FRIEND--?
DOCTORRR SIVANA?
W-WHAT? WHO ARE YOU?
WHAT DO YOU WANT?
YOU.
WE TAKE YOU NOW LIVE TO METROPOLIS WHERE MORE ARE ARRIVING IN CITY PARK....I SEE THEM. THERE'S A BIG BRIGHT LIGHT IN THE SKY... IT'S--

RAY!
YOU MADE IT! YOU'RE OKAY!
I SURE DID, CANARY.
SORRY TO HEAR ABOUT THE REST OF FREEDOM FIGHTERS.
THE SOCIETY REALLY RIPPED THROUGH US, ARROW.
AND THEY STILL CAN'T FIND UNCLE SAM.
I HEARD RUMORS ABOUT JADE. I FEEL SO BAD FOR ALAN.
NO MAN SHOULD HAVE TO LOSE HIS OWN DAUGHTER.
...YEAH, WALLY'S DOING FINE. HE AND LINDA ARE JUST TAKING SOME TIME AWAY.
YOU SHOULD SEE HOW BIG THE TWINS ARE GETTING.
THOUGH THEY'RE KINDA ANNOYING.
AN' YOU'RE NOT INTERESTED IN BEIN' THE NEXT FLASH, HUH?
LET JAY FILL THE BOOTS AGAIN. MY SPEED'S GONE, WILDCAT.
I JUST WISH I'D BEEN FAST ENOUGH TO SAVE CONNER.
WE ALL DO, BART.
YOU CAN LET GO, BEA.
NOT YET. J'ONN.
DIDN'T YOU SAY RALPH WOULD BE HERE...?
LOOKS LIKE A LOT OF PEOPLE ARE GETTING ACCOUNTED FOR. IT'S...NICE.
SUPERMAN, BATMAN AND WONDER WOMAN ARE DUE TO BEGIN IN LESS THAN A MINUTE, SIR.

...'COURSE WE SAVED THE WORLD. C'MON NOW. WE GOT WONDER WOMAN BACK ON OUR SIDE...
...ASSUME SUPERMAN'S GOING TO GIVE THE EULOGY. HE HAS TO.
AND THEN PROBABLY SOME BIG RAH-RAH SPEECH ABOUT PEACE AND BROTHERHOOD AND ALL THAT CRAP.
YOU'RE THE ONE THAT BROUGHT THE CAMERA, GUY.
SO, WHERE ARE SUPERMAN, BATMAN AND WONDER WOMAN?

...I'D SUGGEST WORKING YOUR WAY TO THE STAGE.
GNN
THEY'LL *BE* HERE, KID. JUST RELAX.
FOUR
THREE SECONDS TO THE *BIG MOMENT*, SIR...
...*TWO*
ONE.

TA-DAAAAAAA--
...?
:KOFF:
WHAT'S HE DOIN', ANNOUNCIN' HIMSELF?
HE WOULD.
WHERE ARE THEY, SKEETS?
THEY SHOU1010001 BE HERE, SIR. THE TIME--
--IS 4:32! AND I DON'T SEE THEM. ANYWHERE!
BOOSTER, A LITTLE DECORUM, PLEASE...?
NO! NO! YOU DON'T UNDERSTAND, J'ONN. SKEETS, CHECK THE RECORDS AGAIN!
I'M PROCESSING THEM AT TERABYTES A PICO011000SECOND, SIR. THEY ALL INDICOO110TE A 4:30 APPEARANCE!
4:35 AND COUNTING, SKEETS! YOUR CLOCK IS OFF!
ATOMIC TIME, SIR! SOMETHING'S WROOO110NG! SOM110THING'S WROOOO--

KZZZTTTTT
SKEETS!
BOOSTER, WILL YOU SETTLE DOWN?
NO! YOU DON'T UNDERSTAND! WHERE ARE THEY?
WHERE THE HELL ARE THEY?
WHERE ARE WHO, BOOSTER?
I'M TALKIN' ABOUT SUPERMAN AND BATMAN, YOU CHUCKHEAD! WONDER WOMAN!
THE FUTURE DEPENDS ON THEM! I KNOW! I'VE SEEN IT! I--
OLSEN?
BOOSTER--!
TAKE THE PICTURE, OLSEN! TAKE THE PICTURE!
THEY'RE HERE! THEY HAVE TO BE HERE!
THIS IS YOUR HOWITZER!
GREAT H'RONMEER, HE'S OUT OF CONTROL! HOLD HIM!
WHERE ARE--?
BOOSTER, THEY'RE NOT COMING! THEY
NNNGH!
KRAK
WHAT DO YOU MEAN THEY'RE NOT COMING?
HOW THE HELL DO YOU KNOW?
I JUST KNOW.
AND I'M SORRY.

Week 1, Day 7

CHAK

I CAN SEE YOU.

I'm halfway through the door and calling out her name before I remember.
DEE?
There's no answer.

Of course there's no answer, she's not coming back. Three months, she's not coming back.
Another partner out of my life.

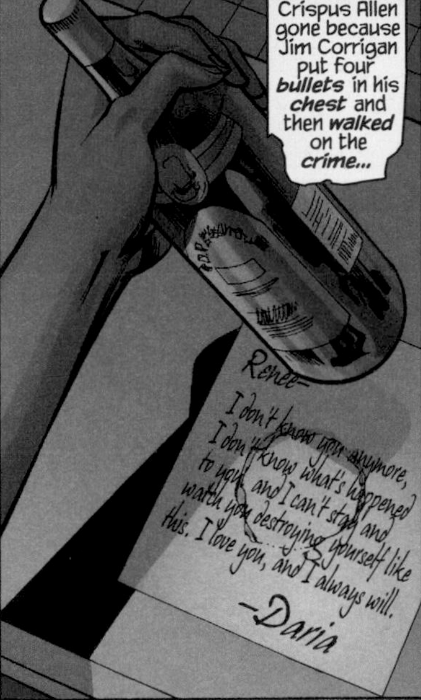
Crispus Allen gone because Jim Corrigan put four bullets in his chest and then walked on the crime...
Renee—
I don't know you anymore,
I don't know what's happened
to you and I can't stay and
watch you destroying yourself like
this. I love you, and I always will.
—Daria

...and Dee too, because I did everything I could to drive her away except show her the door myself....

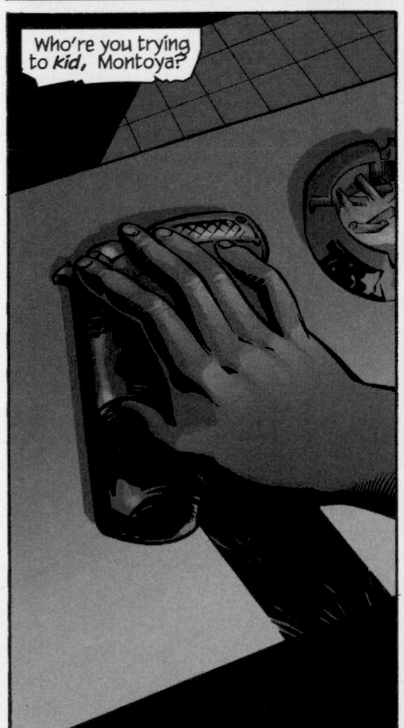
Who're you trying to kid, Montoya?

You're a coward. You couldn't kill Corrigan, you can't...

WHAT THE HELL?

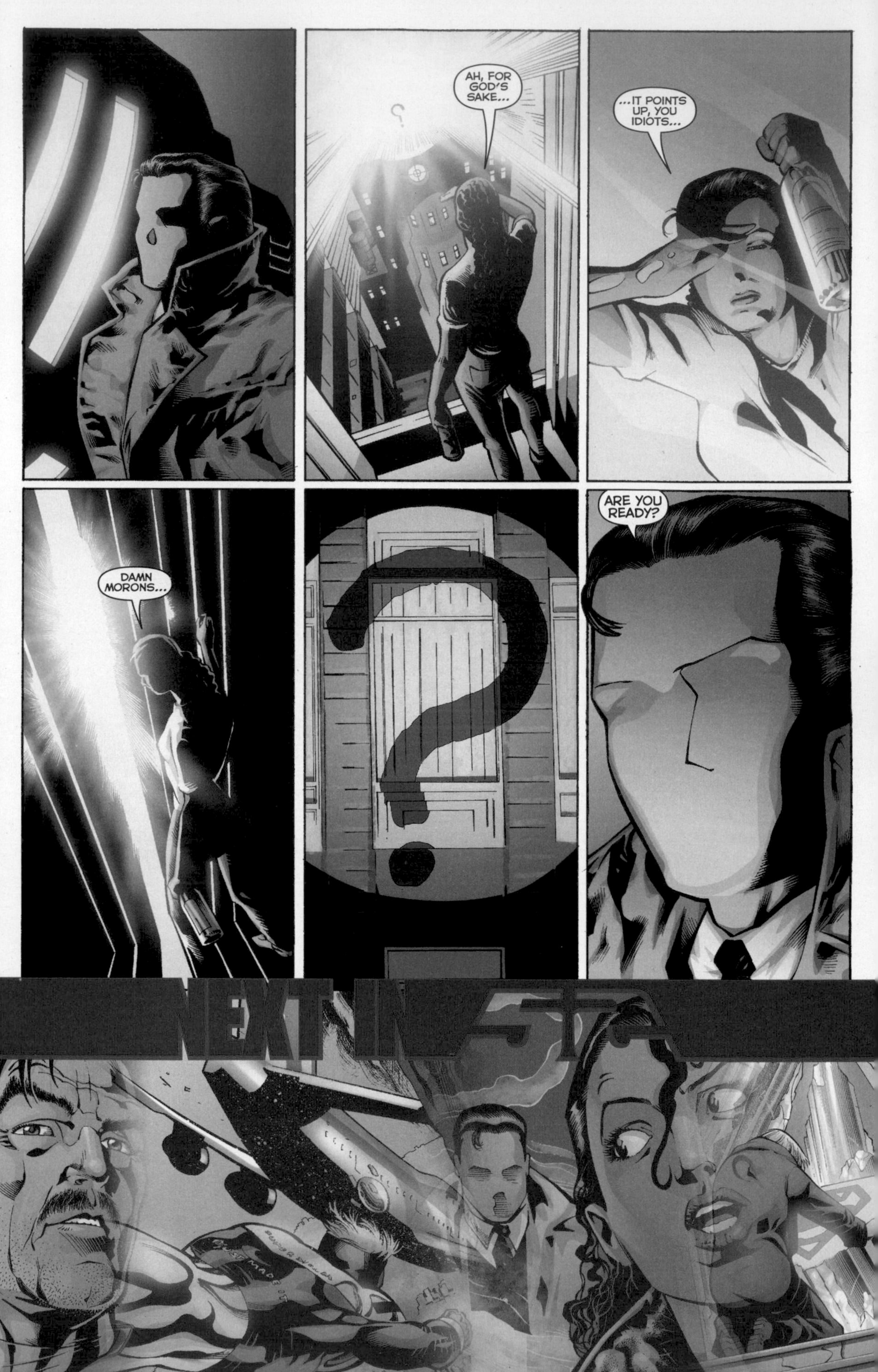
AH, FOR GOD'S SAKE...
...IT POINTS UP, YOU IDIOTS...
DAMN MORONS...
ARE YOU READY?
NEXT IN 52

WEEK ONE NOTES

PAUL LEVITZ

Fragments: Dan, Geoff and Greg in my office, giant flip pad filling with magic marker scribbles... "One Year Later" back on the board, hard to kill...okay, alternatively, raise the bar: if you want OYL, tell the story of the year in a unique vehicle, maybe real time like *24* and "**52**" is uttered for the first time in context. They stagger out, muttering crazy publisher and less kind phrases. Hour later, they're back, rising to the challenge. Half an idea, half a bunch of kids in the schoolyard refusing to let a dare go unanswered. Feeling guilty, I offer to help, get myself into largest writing project since I walked away from the keyboard when my kids were little. Dan bouncing in, again and again, over the next weeks: four writers, team approach stolen from TV, Keith enlisted to keep art consistent (n.b., sigh as I recall racing to feed Jack enough scripts to keep him on pace for his preferred book-a-week pencilling speed in the '70s), concepts that come and go (seasons, holidays, covers influenced by *Time Magazine*), J.G. on board, picking up a pencil to Curtis's cover designs, writers' meetings, marketing meetings, finished issues appearing on my desk.

The accident of how **52** started and its unusual potential impact on the line meant that I was closer to the creative process for this series than any that DC has published in two decades (and that's still up in the bleachers on the sidelines). Close enough to share in the pride at its success, and distant enough that each week's issue has surprised and entertained me as I first read it in print. Now Dan wants annotations for the trade, but where to begin...

Each issue is so rich in DC history, born of so many sources: Elongated Man, created as a Flash supporting character then given his own backup because Julie could use him as the foil for the puzzle stories he loved to plot with writers John Broome and Gardner Fox; Steel, crafted as one of the trick "Superman replacements" when the original died in the '90s; Montoya, from the animated *Batman*, given a more complex life story in her comics appearances; Booster Gold, Dan's creation for a solo title; Black Adam, Sivana and Mister Mind, whose Fawcett publishing history goes back before my birth; the Question from the Charlton line; characters I've written like Huntress; and ones from my childhood, like Metamorpho. A full annotation would take pages, not paragraphs, and I'd need help on the products of the last fertile decades. That task will have to wait for another person, another place.

Let it stand, thus: more than any single DC title before, **52** is a collaboration. Collaboration between a stellar team of DC's current writers, artists and editors. Collaboration between three generations of creators, who added characters to the DC universe for stories they wanted to tell, and ultimately for others to take and transform for later times. Collaboration between people who worked for three different publishing companies, an animation studio, and probably some place else not yet evident in this issue. And collaboration across time, between people who may not have met, or even lived at the same moment...but who all wanted to tell stories to entertain you.

Here's hoping we succeeded.

KEITH GIFFEN

When the first script showed up, I remember thinking, "we pull this off, we make comic book history... we screw it up, we make comic book history." I really wasn't up to becoming the comic book version of that "agony of defeat" guy. One down, fifty one to go. God help us...

MARK WAID

After the entire issue was put together, the vote among us to move the last page to page one (Wacker's idea) was pretty evenly split, and I lobbied hard for it. I still think it's a neat idea.

These "shard" images are what were shown in the opening pages of 52, swirling in the maelstrom. The images not only reveal key moments from the past, but also important events of the future.

THE PROCESS

BREAKDOWNS BY **KEITH GIFFEN**

PENCILS BY **JOE BENNETT**

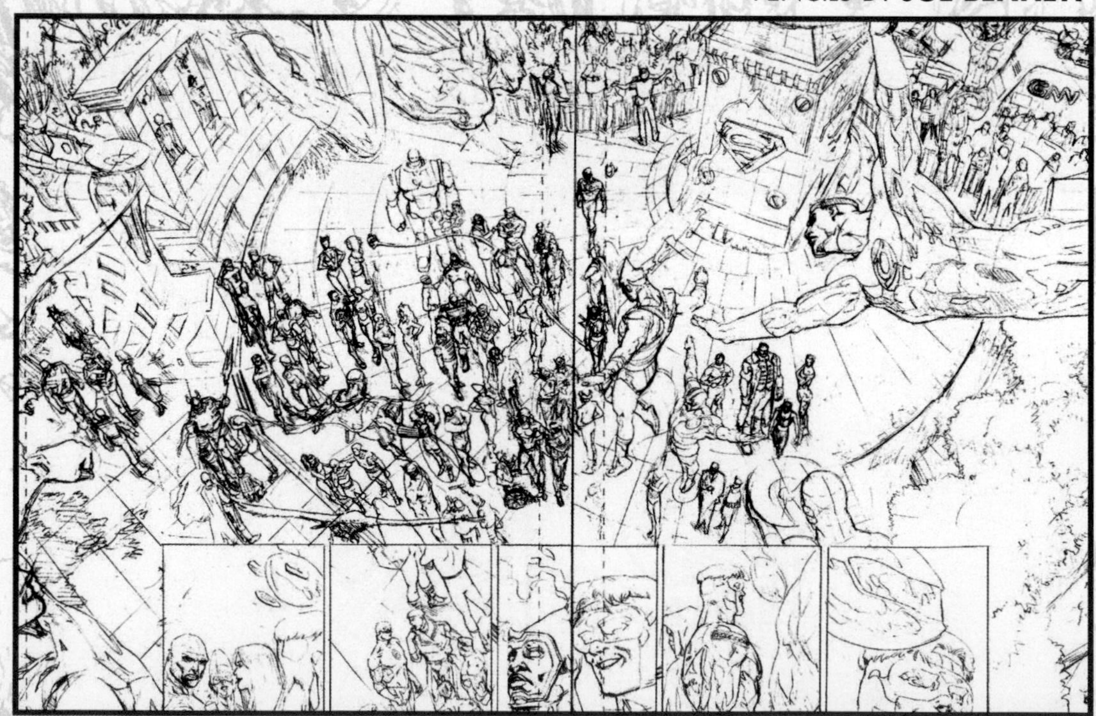

LOOKING BACK AT TOMORROW

OLD-SCHOOL CAMERA.

OLD-FASHIONED DETECTIVE. RALPH DIBNY. AND YOU ARE...?

DUDE, I KNOW. BELIEVE ME. BIG FAN OF THE ELONGATED MAN.

WRITTEN BY GEOFF JOHNS, GRANT MORRISON, GREG RUCKA, MARK WAID

YOU WON'T BELIEVE THIS, BUT I MET YOU AND YOUR WIFE WAY LONG AGO. REMEMBER DREAMLAND PARK?

DO I EVER. I HAD TO FIGURE OUT HOW SOMEONE KIDNAPPED A BOY FROM A MOVING ROLLER COASTER WITHOUT BEING SEEN. WAS THAT YOU?
MY BROTHER. DUDE, YOU WERE AMAZING. LIKE, BATMAN-AMAZING.

BATMAN'S GOOD.
BATMAN DOESN'T HAVE A WIFE WHO KEPT ME FROM FREAKING OUT WHILE YOU WERE TRACKING DOWN MARTY. MY BROTHER MARTY.

BREAKDOWNS BY KEITH GIFFEN • PENCILS BY JOE BENNETT • INKS BY JACK JADSON

COLORS BY ALEX SINCLAIR • LETTERING BY TRAVIS LANHAM

ASSISTANT EDITORS JANN JONES & HARVEY RICHARDS • EDITED BY STEPHEN WACKER
COVER BY J.G. JONES & ALEX SINCLAIR • SPECIAL THANKS TO JOE PRADO

NO CLUES *NEARBY...* I'VE BEEN *LOOKING...*

AND THIS IS EXACTLY HOW YOU *FOUND* IT? YOU'RE THE *GROUNDSKEEPER* HERE?

UH-HUH. HEY, I'M SORRY. I'LL CLEAN THIS UP, KEEP A CLOSER EYE OUT FOR VANDALS.

PARIS. CAIRO. MONTE CARLO.

EXCUSE ME?

THAT'S A TYPICAL WEEK FOR ME EVEN NOW. SUE TAUGHT ME THE JOY OF *WORLD TRAVEL,* SON. WE-- *I--NEVER* STAY IN ONE PLACE FOR *LONG.*

THIS WASN'T A *TOWNIE* WITH A *SPRAY CAN.*

THIS IS SOMEONE LEAVING A *MESSAGE* FOR *ME* THE ONE PLACE THEY *KNOW* I'LL *FIND* IT.

WHO WOULD *DO* THAT?

IT'S A MYSTERY.

Week 2, Day 1

...HE'S NEVER DONE ANYTHING LIKE THIS BEFORE.
MAGNUS
NO PRESSURE BUT I'M RELYING ON THIS LITTLE GUY'S KNOWLEDGE OF THE FUTURE TO DO MY JOB AS A SUPER-HERO.
SKEETS HERE IS A SELF-REPAIRING VALET MODULE FROM THE 25TH CENTURY, MISTER GOLD.
IF THERE'S ANY DAMAGE HERE AT ALL, I CAN'T FIND IT, BUT I'M NO EXPERT ON TOMORROWTECH.
SORRY ABOUT THAT.
WELCOME BACK ONLINE.
DON'T APOLOGIZE, DOCTOR MAGNUS!
IT FELT GREAT TO BE OFF DUTY FOR A LITTLE WHILE!
Y'KNOW THAT WHOLE ZEN THING?
YOU SHOULD TRY IT, SIR!
IN FACT THE WHOLE INTERNET SHOULD TRY IT ONCE A WEEK.
STAR
NO EXPERT? YOU'RE THE 21ST CENTURY'S FOREMOST AUTHORITY ON ANDROID A.I.
YOU'RE STILL FAMOUS IN MY TIME FOR INVENTING THE METAL MEN.

Umm...THOSE DON'T REALLY WORK ANYMORE.
ANYWAY, I'M A LITTLE LATE...
AND MAY I JUST ADD WHAT AN HONOR AND A PRIVILEGE IT IS TO MEET THE FATHER OF THE ARTIFICIAL SELF.
UMM. SURE.
SO HOW D'YOU FEEL?
MY GUESS IS A GLITCH, BOOST.
IT HAD TO BE A GLITCH.
BECAUSE IF IT WASN'T A GLITCH, SOMEBODY IS MESSING WITH THE FABRIC OF TIME.
WE'LL TALK ABOUT THIS LATER.
STILL NEED A RIDE TO HAVEN, DOC?
THAT WOULD BE GREAT.
SEE, I'M ONLY REGARDED AS THE "WORLD'S FOREMOST AUTHORITY" BECAUSE NO ONE WANTS TO ACKNOWLEDGE THE GUY WHO ACTUALLY IS.
HE'S IN HAVEN FOR ATTEMPTING TO START A WAR BETWEEN TWO PARALLEL WORLDS.
I'M THE ONLY ONE WHO VISITS.
AND LIKE I SAID, I'M A LITTLE LATE...

...I RIGGED UP A TACHYON DISH SO THE TV CAN RECEIVE PAP FROM THE FUTURE.
THAT OLD MAN THEY'RE ALL LAUGHING AT IS ASHTON KUTCHER.
WARNING: FORCE FIELD DOME
IN HERE, YOU USE YOUR TALENTS TO SURVIVE ANY WAY YOU CAN.
LOOK AT ME, MY GENIUS MANIFESTED ITSELF IN THE CREATION OF MACHINES SO FULLY CONSCIOUS THEY DEFIED EVEN THEIR MAKER.
YOURS GAVE LIFE TO THOSE SLAVISHLY DEVOTED METAL MEN.
American Science
"NO MORE HEROES"
GAH! WHAT AM I READING HERE? AN HISTORICAL JOURNAL?
YOU AND I, WE'RE MEN WHO HAVE WILLFULLY BROUGHT INTO BEING THINGS THAT JUST DON'T BELONG IN THIS DAY AND AGE.
THINGS OF TOMORROW.
BUT I'M THE MAD SCIENTIST, LOCKED UP FOR MY OWN GOOD AND THE GOOD OF OTHERS.
YOU KNOW THEY WON'T LET ME NEAR A COMPUTER IN CASE I USE IT TO TRIGGER MACHINE WAR ONE.
THAT'S WHAT SOME OF US MEAN WHEN WE TALK ABOUT FIGHTING INJUSTICE, WILL.
SPEAKING OF WHICH, A LOT OF SUPERHEROES WERE KILLED.
THINGS ARE CHANGING OUT THERE.
AND I THOUGHT YOU SHOULD KNOW THE...Ah... RED TORNADO GAVE HIS LIFE..TO PROTECT THE EARTH.

TSSK
WHY DOES HE HAVE TO KEEP DOING THAT?
SOME SELF-DESTRUCTIVE PROGRAMMING FLAW, YOU THINK, OR THE DAWNING OF SYNTHETIC COURAGE ITSELF ?
ONLY ONE OF HIS BROTHERS EVER SHOWED ANYTHING LIKE THE SAME SELF-AWARENESS.
American Science
"NO MORE HEROES"
PERHAPS ONE DAY I'LL TELL YOU ABOUT THE RED INFERNO.
I'M NOT SOME COMMON INVENTOR OR MAKER OF MACHINES!
I'M AN ARTIST.
YOU LAID THE GROUNDWORK FOR EVERYTHING I KNOW ABOUT CYBERNETIC INTELLIGENCE SYSTEMS, PROFESSOR MORROW.
I CAN'T SAY I AGREE WITH HOW YOU'VE DEPLOYED YOUR TALENTS, SIR, BUT I'VE ALWAYS VALUED YOUR FRIENDSHIP.
I WOULDN'T MISS OUR MONTHLY DISCUSSIONS FOR THE WORLD.
I CREATED THE WORLD'S FIRST ARTIFICIAL SOULS, WILL.
YOU'RE THE ONLY ONE OF MY STUDENTS WHO EVER TRULY UNDERSTOOD THE SIGNIFICANCE OF THAT BREAKTHROUGH.
I KNOW YOU'VE BEEN THROUGH A LOT.
I...VERY MUCH APPRECIATE THESE VISITS.

I ALSO KNOW YOU'RE NOT THE KIND TO PAY TOO MUCH ATTENTION TO THE NEWS, WILL.
BUT IN ALL THE FUSS SURROUNDING LEX LUTHOR, IT'S NO SURPRISE A MYSTERIOUS RAID ON SIVANA'S HIDEOUT CAN WIND UP BURIED ON PAGE 10.
THEN THERE WAS THE DISAPPEARANCE FROM HIS UNDERGROUND LABORATORY LAST WEEK OF IRA QUIMBY, A.K.A. I.Q.
JOINING DOCTORS DEATH, TYME AND CYCLOPS ON THE RECENT "MISSING" FILES.
YOU KNOW WHAT I THINK ?
I THINK SOMEONE'S ROUNDING US UP.
"US"?
SCIENTISTS?
ZENITH CITY ZENITH
DR CYCLOPS JOINS THE "EVIL BRAIN DRAIN"
"Local supervillain 'missing for days' says bartender friend"
CRIMINAL MASTERMIND SKIPS BAIL, LEAVES LOOT
Has IRA 'I.Q.' Quimby outsmarted himself ?
GOTHAM TIMES
MYSTERY OF THE WANDERING WITNESS
CURSES! FOILED AGAIN!'
FBI raid finds Marvel family nemesis lab empty
MAD SCIENTISTS, WILL.
HA
'THE STRANGE CASE
DOCTOR TYME
"MAD DOCTOR" JEREMIAH CLUGG VANISHES FROM RENTED LAIR
Neighbors talk of "snarling sounds"
Jeremiah Clugg, local scientist and supposedly 'mad' doctor has apparently vanished from the lair he has been renting
IF I WERE YOU, I'D WATCH MY STEP.
AND KEEP TAKING MY ANTI-DEPRESSANTS.

Week 2, Day 3
PIZZA
"NO MORE HEROES"
WHO ARE YOU?

BLAM
BLAM
AAHHH!
OHMYGOD OHMYGOD HE DOESN'T HAVE A FACE OH MY--
SHUT UP!

WH-WHERE'D HE GO?
YOU SHOT HIM, RIGHT? YOU-YOU HIT HIM?
DO YOU SEE HIM? DID YOU GET HIM?
WHAT DO WE DO? DO WE CALL THE COPS?
RENEE?
5:20
WHAT IS IT? RENEE!
RENEE, C'MON, YOU'RE FREAKING ME OUT...
...RENEE...?
...Uhm, HELLO...?
520 Kane St
?
PUT SOME CLOTHES ON.

Week 2, Day 4
MAYDAY! MAYDAY! METROPOLIS TOWER, WE HAVE EXPERIENCED A MAJOR INSTRUMENTATION MALFUNCTION! ENACT EMERGENCY LANDING PROTOCOL 2X-2L!
TOWER? TOWER, THIS IS FLIGHT 2824 DO YOU READ?
SIR! THERE'S A FALLING JETLINER COMING IN FROM THE NORTH!
THIS LOOKS LIKE A JOB FOR BOOSTER GOLD!
I'M ON IT, SKEETS!
THE JET'S FLIGHT PATH IS A MATTER OF HISTORICAL RECORD, SO YOU'RE POSITIONED PERFECTLY! IMPACT--
SPEAK UP! I CAN'T HEAR YOU OVER THE WIND!
--IMPACT IN FIVE SECONDS, SIR! YOUR FORCE-DAMPERS ARE FULLY CHARGED! BRACE YOURSELF!
FOR WHAT?
YOU SAID NORTH, RIGHT?

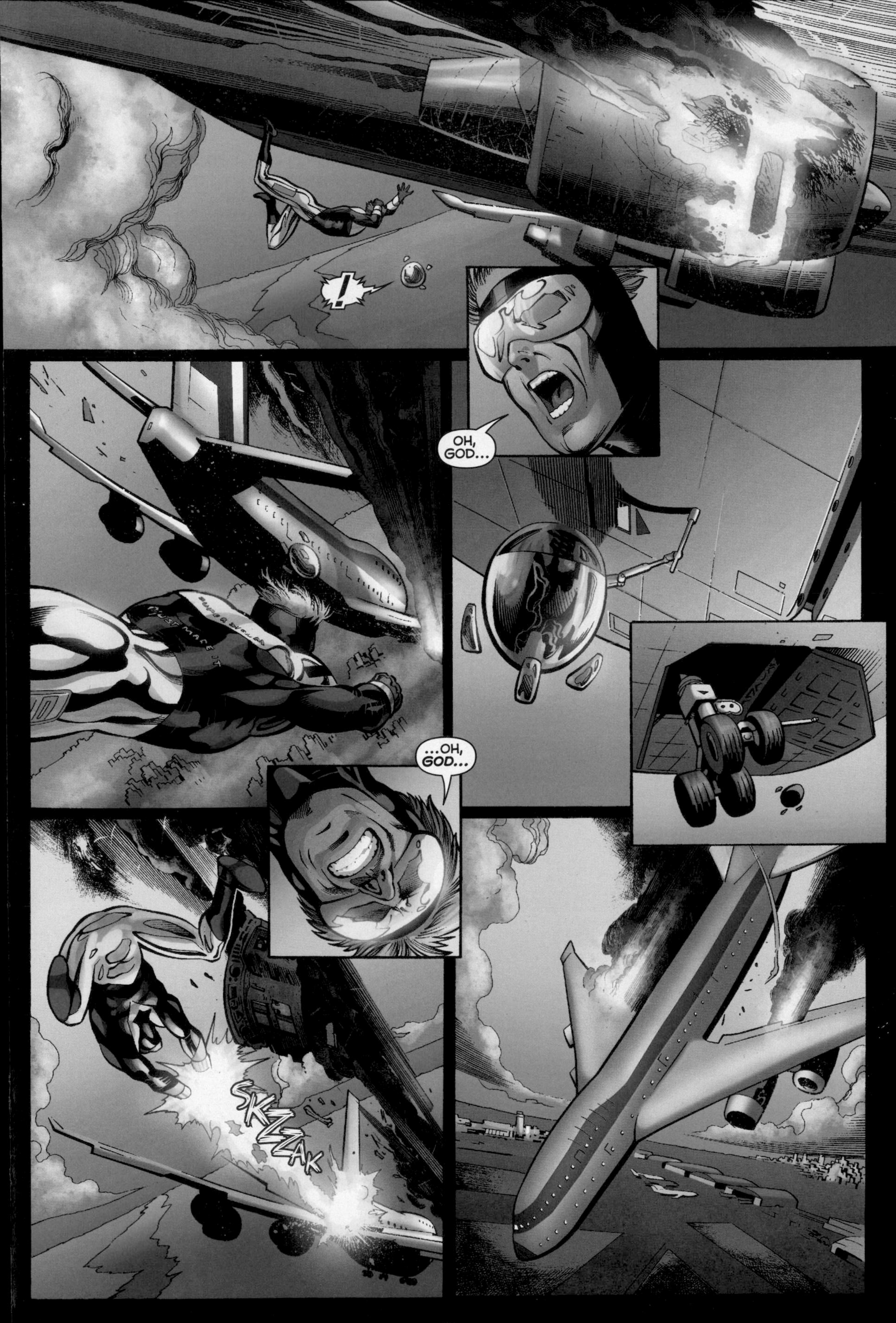
!
OH, GOD...
...OH, GOD...
SKZZZAK

FUMP
CHARLIE, HERE'S YOUR HEADLINE: "BOOSTERRIFIC!"
RIGHT WITH YOU FOLKS! JUST GIVE ME A MOMENT TO...REFLECT ON OUR LUCK.
BOOSTER, CAN WE GET A QUOTE?
BOOSTER? CHANNELSEVEN NEWS!
SIR, IT WASN'T LUCK--
NO KIDDING! "NORTH"? WHAT THE HELL--? GET MAGNUS ON THE LINE! TELL HIM YOU'RE STILL FRAGGED!
NO NEED, SIR. MY APOLOGIES. MERELY A LAST, RESIDUAL GLITCH IN MY SELF-CORRECTIVE PROGRAMMING. ALL'S WELL NOW.
FLIGHT 2824 IS JUST FINE NOW.
The Sydney Mornin
HUNDREDS DEAD O
FLIGHT 2428

Memory, that's the problem.
Or more precisely, the fact that I have one, and worse, that it's a damn good one.
Fantastic when you're trying to remember where you parked...
...Not so good when you're doing everything you can to forget the car crash you've made of your life.
The no-face guy...what the hell was that about?
Vanished like he was never here, and I know I hit him dead center.
Asking me who I am, son of a bitch can join the club.
He'll get the same answer Daria got...
Renee–
I don't know you anymore, i don't know what's happened to you, and I can't stay and watch you destroying yourself like this. I love you, and I always will.
–Daria
520 Kane St
...I don't know.
I haven't got a goddamn clue.

PRIVATE PROPERTY— KEEP OUT!
520
Mystery solved.
It's an abandoned building.
There you go, curiosity satisfied.
Man with no face surprises you in the middle of the night, vanishes after being shot, leaves mystery address.
Nothing at the address.
Fine, done, time to get back to the important work of drinking oneself into oblivion--
KIND OF A DUMP, ISN'T IT?
SON OF A--
KRRSH
UNNH!

DO YOU SHOOT EVERYONE YOU MEET, OR IS THIS A PERSONAL THING?
WHO THE HELL ARE YOU?
I ASKED YOU FIRST.
I SHOT YOU, I KNOW I SHOT YOU.
ARE YOU SURE?
PRETTY SURE.
SO YOU ARE A DETECTIVE AFTER ALL.
NO, I'M NOT. I'VE GOT A NEW JOB, IT'S CALLED BEING A DRUNK.
100
100
DO I JUDGE YOU BY WHAT YOU SAY OR BY WHAT YOU DO, RENEE?
HOW DO YOU KNOW MY NAME?
I'M HIRING YOU. TWO HUNDRED A DAY PLUS EXPENSES...
...FIRST THREE WEEKS PAID IN ADVANCE.
DON'T JUDGE THE BUILDING BY HOW IT LOOKS...
...JUDGE IT BY HOW IT'S USED AND BY WHO USES IT....
WHAT? WAIT!
DAMMIT--
--I STILL HAVE QUESTIONS!

...AND EVEN AS KRYPTON'S RED SUN DIMS IN THE EVENING SKIES, KNOW...AND *REMEMBER...*
Week 2, Day 6
...THAT IT IS BY THE STRENGTH OF OUR *FAITH* AND OUR *LOVE* THAT YOUR PATH STAYS AS *BRIGHT* AS THE EYES OF LADY KANDOR *HERSELF.*
SO SAY WE *ALL.*
SO SAY WE *ALL.*
SO SAY WE *ALL.*
WEBCAST LIVE, SUPERBOY 4EVER!
<SO SAY WE *ALL.*>
<SO SAY WE *ALL.*>
TRANSMISSION *ENDED.*
KLIK

I HEAR HE LOVED YOU, TOO, CASSIE. WONDER GIRL, IF YOU'RE STILL CALLING YOURSELF THAT.
WHO--?
RALPH DIBNY. WE'VE MET.
A FEW DAYS AGO SOMEONE DEFACED MY WIFE'S GRAVESTONE WITH WHAT I HAVE REASON TO THINK WAS A MESSAGE FROM YOU.
M-MESSAGE? I--WHY WOULD YOU--?
BECAUSE YOU DID YOUR HOMEWORK. THE ALTAR, THE CRYSTALS... VERY AUTHENTIC. SEE, I DID MY RESEARCH, TOO.
THE "S," CASSIE. NOT MANY PEOPLE KNOW THAT IT HAD LITERAL MEANING. IT'S A SYMBOL.

ON KRYPTON, IT TRANSLATED AS THE WORD *"HOPE."*
INVERTED, THOUGH, IT STANDS FOR SOMETHING ELSE *ALTOGETHER:*
RESURRECTION.
SUE
NEXT IN

WEEK TWO NOTES

DAN DIDIO

My first thought was, "Wow, only 50 more to go."

With so much pre-planning and so much at stake, it felt great to hold the second issue in my hands. The funny thing is that writers, working with Editorial, spent the last several months breaking down and "re-breaking down" the story so that we would have a comprehensive outline for all 52 issues, yet here we were with the second issue and the writing team was already coming up with things anew. The beat with Ralph and the Resurrection Cult was a late addition to the outline. This was a sign of things to come.

The four writers, rather than working on individual scripts as originally planned, decided that they would work on every issue together, each taking a certain allotment of pages in every issue to tell their portion of the story. This left me scratching my head wondering if this was the best course of action, but they were fully committed to doing this and more important, they were on a roll. But with all four writing each issue, they all participated in a weekly conference call to break down the next issue and as time went on, the stringent plot became a little more fluid and the creative process took over. Some things changed and, more important, some things remained the same.

By the second issue you get several hints of things to come and stories that would not see their conclusion until the final issues. T.O. Morrow talks of missing scientists to Doc Magnus (every missing scientist on Morrow's board appears later in the series) and we see the first sign that there might be something wrong with Skeets (but we didn't know how wrong until a later writers' meeting).

We also wanted to try something on the covers. The original idea was to try to put an "Easter egg" on each cover. You know, some little hidden secret that comes into play in a later issue. It was quickly abandoned when we realized that JG's covers were so dynamic in their own right, this idea would seem forced. We agreed that we should only do it when it was appropriate. But on this cover, the keen eyes of thousands of fans noticed a rather reserved Clark Kent standing behind a "very happy" Booster Gold. This helped convey an important twist — we promised a year without Batman, Superman and Wonder Woman, but by showing Clark, it gave the fans a heads-up that their favorite characters might still appear, but just not in a way they would expect them.

Superman may be gone,
but Clark Kent is still around.
BOOSTER GOLD CLUB

BREAKDOWNS

BY **KEITH GIFFEN**

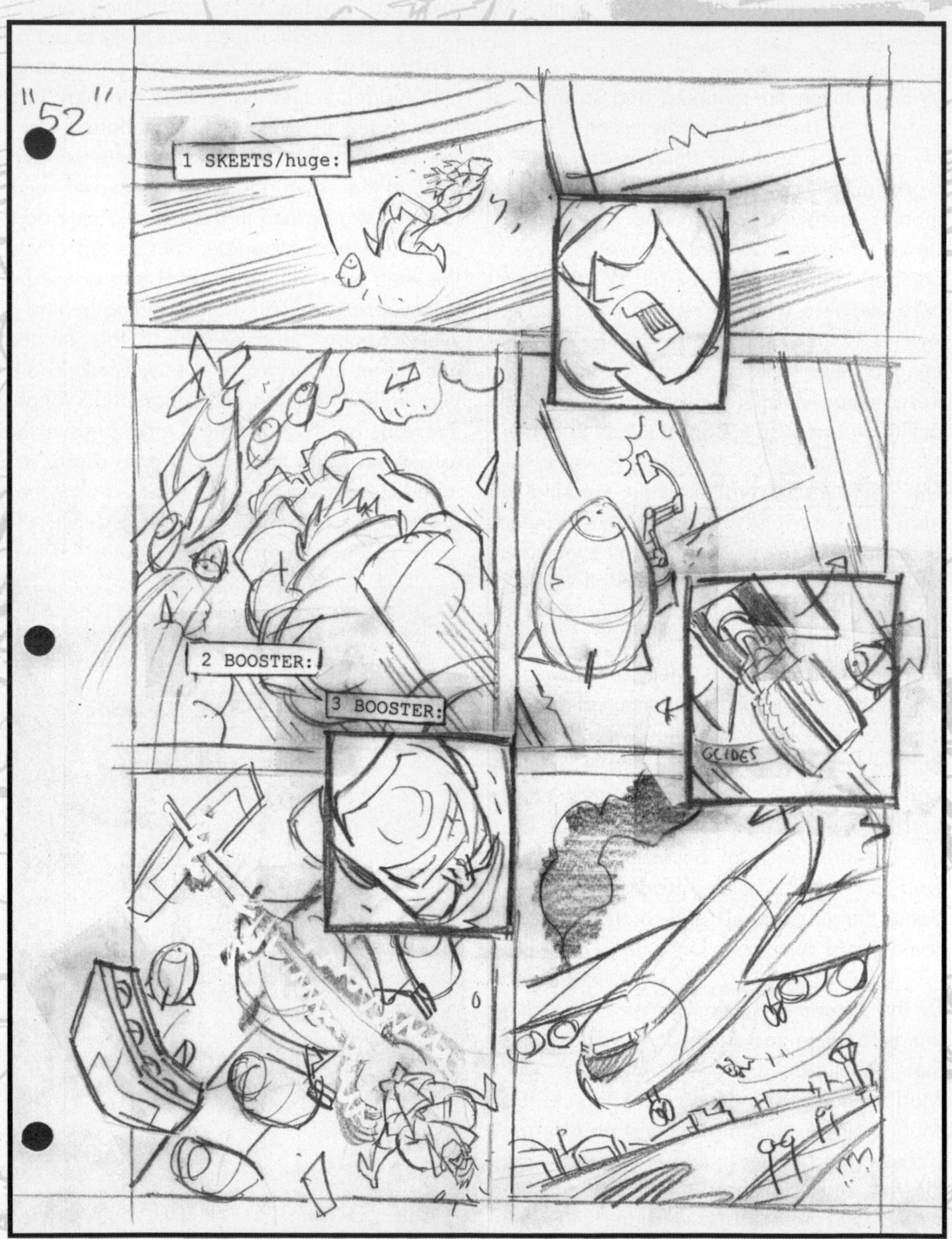

Booster tries to save a falling jetlinet from crashing.
Compare Keith Giffen's original breakdowns here to the final version on page 45.

Week 3, Day 1
Gotham City.
CAPTAIN SAWYER! OVER HERE!
WALLIS, MAKE SURE YOU GET A SHOT OF THIS...
SURE THING, DETECTIVE MacDONALD.
DETECTIVE JIANG.
PLEASE TELL ME WHY YOU'VE BROUGHT ME DOWN HERE IN THE MIDDLE OF THE NIGHT TO LOOK AT ANOTHER GOTHAM CORPSE.
YEAH, SORRY ABOUT CALLING YOU AT HOME, MAGGIE...
...BUT I DIDN'T WANT TO PUT THE CALL OVER THE RADIO.
THIS HITS, THE MEDIA'S GONNA HAVE A FIELD DAY.
SO WHAT DO YOU HAVE, JOSIE?
WELL, WE COULD BE WRONG, CAPTAIN...
...BUT IT LOOKS LIKE THE FORMER PRESIDENT OF THE UNITED STATES...
...IT LOOKS LIKE LEX LUTHOR...

YEEEEE-HAW!!

Z-TOOM

A REDNECK WHO CAN *FLY.*

DC COMICS 52

YOU KNOW, I'D ALMOST *PAY* TO KNOCK YOU *OUT.*

AW, SHOOT. NOW LOOK WHAT YA GONE AND DONE!

BOOOM

IT'S OVER, TERRA-MAN.

WRITTEN BY GEOFF JOHNS, GRANT MORRISON, GREG RUCKA, MARK WAID

ART BREAKDOWNS BY KEITH GIFFEN · PENCILS BY JOE BENNETT · INKS BY RUY JOSE

COLORS BY ALEX SINCLAIR · LETTERING BY PAT BROSSEAU · COVER BY J.G. JONES & SINCLAIR

ASSISTANT EDITORS JANN JONES & HARVEY RICHARDS EDITED BY STEPHEN WACKER
BUT IT DON'T MEAN I AIN'T UP FOR WATCHIN' YOU SWEAT A LITTLE FIRST.
VZZZATTT!!
AAAHH!
YA KNOW WHAT I HEARD?
NEW WORLD ORDER
Week 3 Week 3 Week 3 Week 3 Week 3 Week 3 Week
AH HEARD YOU WERE A PART A' THAT MESS THAT ALMOST TORE APART THE PLANET. ALL THEM EARTHS IN THE SKIES AND WHAT NOT.
YER FROM ONE OF THEM OTHER EARTHS, RIGHT?
YER SOME STRANGE VISITOR.
YER SUPERGIRL-LITE.
RRRAARRRPP!
CHOOOM
NNNFF.
AND "YER" ABOUT TO BE IN A COMA, COWBOY.
POWER GIRL...

STOP.
BLACK ADAM?
TERRA-MAN JUST ROBBED FERRIS AIR FLIGHT 450 OVER THE MIDDLE OF THE MEDITERRANEAN SEA.
AND NOW YOU ARE OVER THE NORTHEAST OF AFRICA.
KAHNDAQ'S AIRSPACE.
I WILL NOT TOLERATE IT.
YOU WON'T...?
THIS IDIOT ALMOST KILLED A HUNDRED AND FIFTY PASSENGERS ON THAT PLANE. HE'S A STRAGGLER FROM THE SECRET SOCIETY.
THAT CONGLOMERATE OF VILLAINS THAT YOU HELPED SHEPHERD. THAT IS, UNTIL THEY BETRAYED YOUR ASS.
LUTHOR BETRAYED ME.
THERE.
TELESCOPIC VISION'S GOT BUTCH CASSIDY.

HEY--
HOW MANY PEOPLE DIED?
NO ONE. GREEN LANTERN AND STARGIRL STABILIZED THE PLANE--
NOT *TODAY*...
...DURING THE CRISIS.
HOW MANY PEOPLE *DIED?*
I...I DON'T KNOW.
MILLIONS.
FIVE MILLION, SEVENTY-NINE THOUSAND, FOUR HUNDRED AND THIRTY-TWO.
YOU HELPED ALL OF US TAKE ON THE SOCIETY IN METROPOLIS. YOU--
I DID WHAT I HAD TO DO TO PROTECT MY PEOPLE.
AND THEY ARE PROTECTED. NOW IT'S TIME FOR SOMETHING MORE.
YOU'RE GOING TO LET *MORE* DIE IF YOU DON'T LET ME--
IF YOU DO NOT LEAVE IN TEN SECONDS, I WILL CONSIDER YOU TO BE TRESPASSING, AND UNLIKE SO MANY SHEEP IN THIS WORLD...
...TRESPASSES ARE SOMETHING I DO NOT FORGIVE.
TELL YOUR FRIENDS.

Week 3, Day 2
Metropolis—The Steelworks.
UNCLE JOHN...?
HMM?
...THE REGISTRATION CAME FOR THE FUTURE TECH COLLOQUIUM NEXT WEEK. YOU NEED TO CALL THEM.
PROBLEM?
YEAH, PROBLEM!
YOU'RE REGISTERED, I'M NOT.
THEY SCREWED UP.
NO, THAT SOUNDS RIGHT...
...YOU'RE NOT ATTENDING.
WHAT? WHY?
YOU HAVE SCHOOL THAT DAY.
HEL-LO? SCHOOL JUST ENDED, UNCLE JOHN.
YOU'RE LOOKING AT A HIGH SCHOOL SENIOR NOW.
SUMMER SCHOOL, NATASHA.
THAT "D" YOU GOT IN ENGLISH DOESN'T WASH.
ARE YOU $¢%ING KIDDING ME?
WATCH YOUR LANGUAGE, YOUNG LADY.

NO WAY! NO WAY I'M SPENDING SIX WEEKS WITH A BUNCH OF DELINQUENTS PLAYING CATCH UP, UNCLE JOHN!
I'M LIKE EIGHTY I. Q. POINTS SMARTER THAN THOSE LOSERS!
THEN YOU SHOULD HAVE THOUGHT OF THAT BEFORE YOU BLEW OFF ENGLISH THIS YEAR.
IT'S ENGLISH! C'MON, I ACED PHYSICS, I ACED A.P. CHEM, I ACED--
TRIG, AND CALC, YES, I KNOW, YOU'RE BRILLIANT AT THE SCIENCES.
EVERYTHING THAT CAME EASILY TO YOU, YOU ACED.
JUST BECAUSE THERE'S WORK YOU DON'T WANT TO DO DOESN'T MEAN IT DOESN'T NEED DOING.
RINNGG RINNGG
POETS DO POETRY, I'M A SCIENTIST! I'VE GOT MORE IMPORTANT THINGS TO DO THAN READ A BUNCH OF BOOKS BY DEAD WHITE GUYS!
RINNGG RINNGG
YOUR PROBLEM IS THAT YOU'VE GOT BRAINS BUT NO WISDOM. THE FIRST WAS GIVEN TO YOU...
...BUT THE SECOND HAS TO BE EARNED WITH TIME, AND YOU'RE TOO IMPATIENT FOR YOUR OWN GOOD.
STEELWORKS, JOHN HENRY IRONS SPEAKING.
JOHN? IT'S DOCTOR AVASTI AT S.T.A.R.*
ANY CHANCE YOU COULD COME DOWN HERE?
* SCIENTIFIC TECHNOLOGICAL ADVANCED RESEARCH
THE NX-520 GIVING YOU GRIEF AGAIN?
NOT QUITE...
...I NEED YOUR HELP IDENTIFYING A BODY...

Week 3, Day 3
Kahndaq.
<BLACK ADAM.>
<YOU HAVE VISITORS.>
<WHO ARE THEY?>
WE'RE FRIENDS.
YOU SPEAK ARABIC.
I'M NOT JUST BRAWN. THE NAME IS ROUGH HOUSE. THIS IS NOOSE.
IT'S A PLEASURE, YOUR HIGHNESS.
I'M NOT A KING.
REGARDLESS, WE'VE COME HERE TO OFFER YOU GIFTS.
TWO MILLION IN AFRICAN GOLD.
AND THE MOST BEAUTIFUL VIRGIN IN ALL OF EGYPT. GUARANTEED.
MAY I ASK WHY YOU HAVE BROUGHT ME "GIFTS"?
TO CONGRATULATE YOU ON THE OPENING OF YOUR EMBASSY IN NEW YORK...
...AND TO SAY HELLO ON BEHALF OF OUR EMPLOYERS.
INTERGANG.

THE WORLD IS STILL RECOVERING FROM CHAOS. MY BOSSES ARE LOOKING TO TAKE ADVANTAGE OF THAT.
THEY'RE LOOKING TO EXPAND BEYOND NORTH AMERICA.
KAHNDAQ IS ESSENTIALLY THE BRIDGE BETWEEN AFRICA AND THE MIDDLE EAST--
--AND THERE'RE A LOT OF PEOPLE WILLING TO PAY TRUCKLOADS FOR THE KIND OF WEAPONS INTERGANG CAN SUPPLY. THANAGARIAN. APOKOLIPTIAN.
WE'RE MORE THAN WILLING TO CUT YOU IN ON THE ACTION IN EXCHANGE FOR, WHAT SHALL WE CALL IT?
--SAFE PASSAGE.
<LET ME GO, MONSTERS!>
HEY--!
--DAMMIT. HOLD STILL! HOLD STILL, YOU STUPID--
NOOSE!
DON'T DAMAGE HIS GIFT.
SO.
WHAT DO YOU SAY?

W--
SPLOTCH
I SAY NO.
HEY, ADAM.
I LIKE YOUR STYLE.

GIVE UP NOW, SHOCKWAVE, BEFORE ANYONE GETS HURT!
YOU REALLY THOUGHT YOU COULD ROB THE GOLD RESERVE FROM SEWER LEVEL? NOT WHILE I'M IN TOWN!
NOT CERTAIN EVERY REPORTER HEARD THAT BITE, SIR.
NOT WHILE I'M IN TOWN!
BETTER.
I HATE THIS GUY. HE FIGHTS DIRTY, HIS ARMOR SMELLS, AND HE'S A CARDINALS FAN.
YOU DID PUT ME DOWN FOR THE METEORS TODAY, RIGHT?
AFFIRMATIVE, SIR. HISTORICAL DATA SHOWS THAT THEY ACHIEVE VICTORY 5-4. TRUST ME AND FIGHT.
LADIES AND GENTLEMEN, BOYS AND GIRLS, CHILDREN OF ALL AGES...
...BE SURE TO TELL YOUR FRIENDS AND LOVED ONES THAT YOU WERE HERE! TODAY! IN PERSON! TO WITNESS THE HEROISM OF BOOSTER GOLD, THE ALL-NEW MAN OF TOMORROW!
BOOSTER GOLD, CHAMPION OF THE WEAK AND THE OPPRESSED!

...TOP OF THE NINTH WITH THE SCORE TIED 4-4, THE METEORS' JOSE JUAREZ STEPS UP TO THE PLATE, ZACHARY EDWARD PITCHING FOR THE CARDINALS...
SEÑOR GYRO
SIR, YOU MIGHT WISH TO MOVE YOUR CART.
GYRO?
CART.
GYRO?
SIGH
I APPRECIATE THAT THIS IS AN INTERRUPTION TO YOUR OBVIOUSLY HECTIC WORKDAY, SIR--
NO GYRO?
--BUT YOU'LL THANK ME IN APPROXIMATELY FOUR SECONDS. THREE... TWO...
SEÑOR GYRO
Week 3, Day 4
Metropolis.

BOOSTER GOLD, KEEPING THE STREETS OF METR--
--MAKE THAT THE PEOPLE OF METROPOLIS--SAFE!
≈PHWOO!≈
MAN, THIS GUY WAS TOUGHER THAN HE--
SIR? WHAT IS IT?
THE BALL GAME, SKEETS. HOW MUCH OF MY MONEY, AGAIN, DID YOU PUT ON IT?
A CONSIDERABLE SUM, SIR. WHY?
BECAUSE IT WOULD REALLY SUCK NOT TO BE RICH. WELL DONE, YOU LITTLE 25TH-CENTURY DATABANK, YOU.
NOW, SHAKE A FIN. WE'RE DUE DOWNTOWN...
...METEORS OVER CARDINALS, 5-4...
SEE YOU AT CAMERA! CANYON!
"...FOR A VERY IMPORTANT AUTOGRAPH SESSION."
ON BEHALF OF AKTEON-HOLT, AMERICA'S LEADER IN PHARMACEUTICALS, I WANT TO SAY HOW PROUD WE ARE TO HAVE THE ENDORSEMENT OF ONE OF THE GREATS OF THE SUPER-HERO WORLD!
THANK YOU, BOOSTER!
TOGETHER, AKTEON-HOLT AND BOOSTER GOLD ARE EAGER TO MAKE YOUR WORLD A BETTER ONE--AND THAT'S WORTH CELEBRATING!
Booster Gold
CLK
CLK

TO THE FUTURE, MR. GOLD...AND TO STOCK OPTIONS THAT WILL MAKE YOU A BILLIONAIRE ONCE WE GO PUBLIC.
WHAT MADE YOU SO CERTAIN A RELATIVELY SMALL COMPANY LIKE MINE WAS WORTH YOUR TIME?
SKEETS. I WAS ON THE LOOKOUT FOR A NEW SPONSOR, MR. AKTEON, AND HE RECOMMENDED YOU AS A MAN ON THE RISE.
SHAME.
MR. AKTEON? AGENT ROGERS, SECRET SERVICE.
YOU'RE UNDER ARREST FOR SECURITIES FRAUD.
WHAT? THERE--THERE MUST BE SOME MISTAKE--!
YEAH. YOURS. THE S.E.C. HAS HAD YOU UNDER OBSERVATION FOR SOME TIME NOW, AND THEIR CASE IS OPEN-AND-SHUT.
SO MUCH FOR "AKTEON-HOLT." HOPE YOU DIDN'T SPEND A LOT ON LETTERHEAD. PARTY'S OVER.
YOU...
...YOU...
SIR, I-- I DON'T--
--THAT WASN'T SUPPOSED TO HAPPEN!
PERHAPS I AM MALFUNCTIONING! SHALL I ATTEMPT TO CONTACT DR. MAGNUS FOR REPAIRS?
NO. I WANT YOU TO FIND SOMEONE ELSE FOR ME.
GET ME EVERYTHING YOU CAN ON THE CURRENT WHEREABOUTS OF A MAN NAMED HUNTER.
RIP HUNTER.

Week 3, Day 5
KALA...
...YOU TAKE A LOOK AT HIS EYES?
HE'S WEARING CONTACTS...
...COLORED CONTACTS...
LEX LUTHOR'S EYES ARE GREEN, NOT BLUE.
THIS ISN'T OUR LUTHOR, KALA. MY GUESS IS THAT THIS IS HIS DOPPEL-GANGER...
...ONE OF THE TROUBLE-MAKERS WHO CAME THROUGH FROM A PARALLEL DIMENSION.
IT WOULD EXPLAIN THE DNA MATCH. IT'S VIRTUALLY IDENTICAL.
SPOTLESS.
WHAT?
THE CONTACTS ARE SPOTLESS, THERE'S NO VISIBLE SIGN OF WEAR ON THEM.
LET'S TAKE A CLOSER LOOK AT HIS EYES. IF HE WAS WEARING CONTACTS FOR A PROLONGED LENGTH OF TIME, THERE'D BE SCARRING ON THE CORNEAS.
YOU THINK THEY WERE INSERTED POSTMORTEM?
WOULDN'T PUT IT PAST HIM.
WOULDN'T PUT IT PAST WHO?
YOU WANT YOUR PROOF?
HIM.

LADIES AND GENTLEMEN OF THE PRESS, YOU HAVE QUESTIONED MY ACTIVITIES, MY ACTIONS, MY VERY CHARACTER AND INTEGRITY.
YOU HAVE DEMANDED EXPLANATIONS AND INVESTIGATIONS INTO MY ACTIVITIES BOTH DURING MY PRESIDENCY AND AFTER.
MANY OF YOU HAVE QUESTIONED MY VERY SANITY.
TIME AND AGAIN I HAVE PROTESTED MY INNOCENCE, AND TIME AND AGAIN YOU AND YOUR VIEWERS, YOUR READERS, HAVE DEMANDED PROOF.
YOU HAVE DEMANDED AN EXPLANATION, AND FOR REASONS THAT WILL BECOME APPARENT, I HAVE BEEN UNABLE TO PROVIDE YOU WITH ONE.
UNTIL NOW.
HELLO, JOHN.
GET IT OVER WITH, LEX.
I TRUST YOU FOUND AND REMOVED THE CONTACTS?
GO TO HELL.
STARLOR VISITOR
LADIES AND GENTLEMEN, EARLIER THIS WEEK, A BODY WAS DISCOVERED IN GOTHAM CITY.
THE BODY OF THIS MAN--

LEX LUTHOR!
LEX! LEX!
WHAT THE HELL?
JUST LIKE HIM, EXACTLY LIKE HIM--
--SAYING THIS MAN WAS IMPERSONATING YOU?

THE EXPLANATION IS LONG, BUT THE QUICK VERSION IS SIMPLY THIS: THE MAN YOU SEE LYING HERE IS ME, BUT FROM ANOTHER REALITY.
A REALITY WHERE LEX LUTHOR WAS A MAN OF MADNESS, NOT OF BUSINESS. A REALITY WHERE LEX LUTHOR CARED NOTHING FOR ANYTHING BEYOND HIS OWN DESIRE FOR POWER.

A REALITY WHERE I WAS TRAPPED WHILE THIS MAN RUINED MY NAME, AND THEN TRIED TO BRING ABOUT THE END OF OUR WORLD.
A REALITY I ESCAPED MERE MOMENTS BEFORE IT CEASED TO EXIST.

DON'T TAKE MY WORD FOR IT.
YOU SEE, STANDING BESIDE ME, DOCTOR JOHN HENRY IRONS, KNOWN TO THE WORLD AS STEEL.
ONE OF THE MANY HEROES WHO STOOD IN THE RECENT CRISIS, WHOSE ACTIONS HELPED TO SAVE US ALL.

HE WAS THERE. HE CAN VERIFY WHAT I'M TELLING YOU.
EVEN IF YOU DON'T TRUST ME...

...YOU KNOW YOU CAN TRUST HIM.

...BECOMING ONE OF THE MOST CONTROVERSIAL TOPICS IN TODAY'S NEWS AS THE KAHNDAQ EMBASSY OFFICIALLY OPENS THIS AFTERNOON IN NEW YORK.
Week 3, Day 6
BLACK ADAM, A NATIVE OF THE NORTH AFRICAN COUNTRY, HAS CLAIMED TO HAVE LIVED AND RULED KAHNDAQ DURING THE *FIFTEENTH DYNASTY* AS THE HISTORICAL FIGURE *TETH-ADAM.*
SCHOLARS AND MIDDLE EASTERN LEADERS *DISPUTE* THESE FACTS AND HAVE CALLED BLACK ADAM A *PRETENDER* AND -- FROM THE AMBASSADOR OF BIALYA--"ONE OF TODAY'S GREATEST EVILS."
SWAT
...HEARD RUMORS FROM D.C. THAT HE'S ABOUT TO OPEN UP HIS COUNTRY TO SUPER-VILLAINS. ANYONE WANTED FOR A CRIME GETS A FREE PASS.
WHY WOULD HE DO THAT?
FROM WHAT I KNOW, HE DOESN'T WANT ANYTHING TO DO WITH THEM.
WELL THEN *WHAT* DOES HE WANT, LOIS?
I THINK HE'S GOING TO *TELL* US.

THANK YOU ALL FOR COMING.
OVER THE LAST YEAR, I HAVE REDEDICATED MYSELF TO THE PEOPLE OF KAHNDAQ.
THAT ENDS *TODAY.*

THE WORLD HAS CELEBRATED THE AVERSION OF DISASTER.
THEY HAVE PRAISED THE *HEROES* WHO STOOD UP TO SAVE THEM.
SUPERMAN, BATMAN AND WONDER WOMAN.

BUT WHERE ARE THEY *NOW?*

I HOPE TO GATHER *ALLIES.*
ALLIES WHO WILL DELIVER MESSAGES TO EVERYONE OUT THERE LOOKING TO TAKE *ADVANTAGE* OF THE HEROES' ABSENCE.
THE FIRST MESSAGE IS SIMPLE...

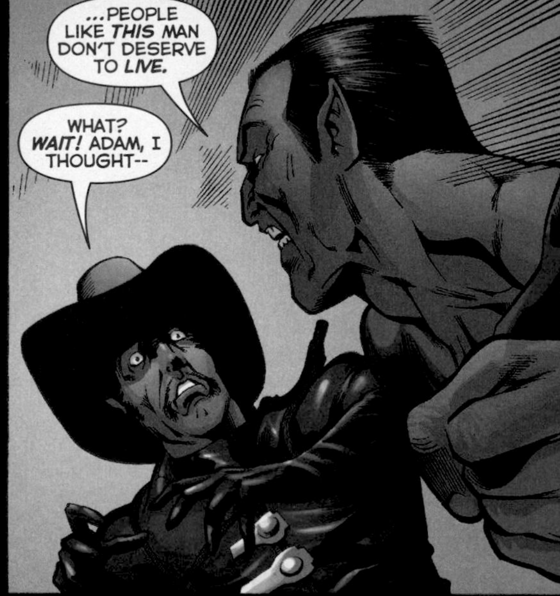
...PEOPLE LIKE *THIS* MAN DON'T DESERVE TO *LIVE.*
WHAT? *WAIT!* ADAM, I THOUGHT--

SHRRAKK
OH, MY GOD!
IT'S TIME FOR HEROES WHO DON'T JUST PATROL THE WORLD...
"...THEY CHANGE IT."
NEXT IN 52

WEEK THREE NOTES

GREG RUCKA

This was an interesting one. After positioning pieces in Weeks 1 and 2, we finally got to give the ball a good shove and get it rolling. Thematically, this week dealt mostly with abuses of power — beginning with the "late" President Luthor and running to Black Adam, with stops for John Henry and Booster in between. In each of these cases, we're seeing people abusing their authority, and in every case the characters perpetrating the abuses feel justified in doing so (or act as such — Booster's performance this week is really a dress rehearsal for the show that will lead to his "unmasking" as a fraud in Week 7). Even John Henry's flexing of muscle — while perhaps justified — certainly drives a deeper wedge between himself and Natasha, and leads directly to their break in Week 8.

Black Adam himself, I think, deserves special mention; his diatribe to Power Girl at the start of the issue is as clear a declaration of his POV as has been written, and reveals one of the things that makes him such a compelling character. He believes in justice, and he believes that having the power to enforce it obligates him to use it — "It's time for heroes who don't just patrol the world. They change it." That he can hold the number of the dead in Crisis so quickly at hand is, again, foreshadowing, but for a payoff much further down the line, and in a much darker way.

Couple of minor notes. In the original script, the two detectives working the crime scene are listed as Josie MacDonald (Josie Mac) and Marcus Driver, both out of GOTHAM CENTRAL. For reasons that have never been made quite clear to me — but I suspect arise from a lack of reference — Driver was drawn as Crispus Allen, a character who was not only dead, but who had become the new host of The Spectre during INFINITE CRISIS. The quick change of name and ethnicity that occurred in the wake of this mistake actually did little to avoid confusion when the issue came out, but ultimately no harm was done. More amusing — or perhaps frustrating — was the magic gyro cart, that dispenses, instead, hot dogs.

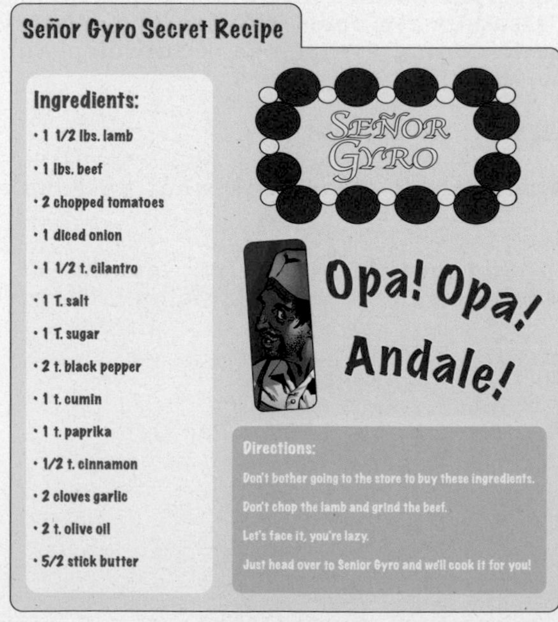

Señor Gyro Secret Recipe
Ingredients:
• 1 1/2 lbs. lamb
• 1 lbs. beef
• 2 chopped tomatoes
• 1 diced onion
• 1 1/2 t. cilantro
• 1 T. salt
• 1 T. sugar
• 2 t. black pepper
• 1 t. cumin
• 1 t. paprika
• 1/2 t. cinnamon
• 2 cloves garlic
• 2 t. olive oil
• 5/2 stick butter
SEÑOR GYRO
Opa! Opa!
Andale!
Directions:
Don't bother going to the store to buy these ingredients.
Don't chop the lamb and grind the beef.
Let's face it, you're lazy.
Just head over to Senior Gyro and we'll cook it for you!

SCRIPT EXCERPT

(COMPARE WITH PAGE 56 OF THIS COLLECTION)

52 WEEK THREE — PAGE TWO

PANEL ONE
Nice big panel. POWER GIRL flies at us at tremendous speed through a beautiful blue sky, chasing TERRA-MAN. Power Girl is her normal, voluptuous self, still recovering from the entire CRISIS. She is mourning the loss of her family inside, taking it out aggressively on super-villains.

Terra-Man is the armored-up version from the recent SUPERMAN comics of the past few years. But let's give him more of a modern-day Old West train-robber-only-he-robs-planes-in-mid-flight-look instead. Terra-Man has sleek, thin body armor underneath a leather jacket, wears a leather cowboy hat strapped to his head, goggles on his eyes. He should have stubble or a mustache or both.

He fires a huge laser gun/cannon back at Power Girl (who dodges it) as he flies off riding a small robotic vehicle — not a horse, but more like a flying motorcycle with the picture of a horse on the side. There is a leather saddle over the flying machine matching his coat and hat. There are also two bags full of his spoils from the plane he just attacked. He's holding on to leather REINS attached to the flying machine.

They're both moving incredibly fast, around 300 mph.

TERRA-MAN: YEEEEE-HAW!!

SFX: Z-TOOM

POWER GIRL: A redneck who can FLY.

POWER GIRL: You know I'd almost PAY to knock you OUT.

PANEL TWO
The heat vision causes the cannon in Terra-Man's hand to EXPLODE. The bags on Terra-Man's saddle rip open, wallets and jewelry — everything he stole from the plane including a snack sack full of peanuts labeled FERRIS AIR — spill out into the air.

SFX: BOOOMMM!

TERRA-MAN: Aw, shoot. Now look what ya gone and done!

PANEL THREE
Terra-Man flies up and over Power Girl, looking at her from upside down avoiding another blast of her heat vision. They're moving at least 300 mph.

POWER GIRL: It's over, Terra-Man.

TERRA-MAN: Hell, I know THAT. Pee Gee.

Week 4, Day 1
Gotham City.
"Bor-ing: adjective, tiresome.
Kane St.
Even when I was on the force, I hated doing surveillance.
It's boring.
It's so boring, it actually redefines boring.
"See also, surveillance."
It's hard on the body, too. seriously, you try sitting in the same position, focusing on the same thing for five, six, even eight hours at a time.
Gives you a whole new appreciation for aspirin, tell you that much.
It also cannot be performed alone, at least not well.
Which means I'm doing a poor job of it, I suppose.
I've been doing a poor job of it for a week, now, and for what?
SUNDOLLER COFFEE
Two hundred a day, plus expenses. First two weeks in advance, paid by the guy with no face.
I took the money, that's the problem.
One week down, one to go...

LIGHTNING THAT CAN'T STRIKE.

DC COMICS 52

MISSION CONTROL TOLD US TO TURN OFF THE TRACKERS AND COME HOME.
THE SEARCH IS OVER.
OFFICIAL.
LIGHTNING THAT CAN'T STRIKE.

WRITTEN BY GEOFF JOHNS, GRANT MORRISON, GREG RUCKA, MARK WAID

ART BREAKDOWNS BY KEITH GIFFEN · PENCILS BY JOE BENNETT
INKS BY JACK JADSON

LIGHTNING THAT CAN'T STRIKE.
WHY DOES SHE KEEP SAYING THAT?
HALO'S FROM AN EXTRADIMENSIONAL WORLD LOCKED INSIDE LIGHT PARTICLES. SHE CAN CREATE, DETECT AND MANIPULATE SUBTLE RADIATION.
SHE'S BEEN SCANNING FOR INCOMING TELEPORTATION WAVES.

COLORS BY ALEX SINCLAIR • LETTERING BY ROB LEIGH
COVER BY J.G. JONES & SINCLAIR

WHAT CAN YOU SEE?
I FOUND AN OSCILLATING SIGNAL WAY UP ON THE ZETA FREQUENCY... TRYING TO COME IN...
ZETA?
ADAM STRANGE TRAVELS BY ZETA BEAM TRANSFER, RIGHT?
HE'S ONE OF OUR M.I.A.s, RIGHT?

ASSISTANT EDITORS JANN JONES & HARVEY RICHARDS • EDITED BY STEPHEN WACKER

GET ME PRESIDENT HORNE.

Week 4

DANCES WITH MONSTERS

Metropolis.
...MORNING THE CITY OF TOMORROW'S OWN BOOSTER GOLD ONCE AGAIN HELPED AVERT DISASTER WHEN SIX-YEAR-OLD THADDEUS STAR FELL FROM AN ELEVATED PLATFORM...

THEY REALLY THINK WE'VE GOT A CHANCE AT FINDING EVERYONE WHO WENT OUT INTO SPACE.

YOU'VE HAD A ROUGH DAY, KID, AND THERE'S ONLY ONE CURE FOR THAT--A BIG BELLY BURGER! IT'S MY FAVORITE SANDWICH IN THE UNIVERSE!
Big Belly Burger
YEAH?
THAT'S GREAT, BEA.

J'ONN IS GETTING A RESCUE TEAM TOGETHER. YOU SHOULD COME.
I WOULD, DEFINITELY, BUT I'VE GOT A SCHEDULE TO KEEP.
WANT A DRINK? I GET BOATLOADS OF THIS STUFF FOR FREE.
WHAT KIND OF SCHEDULE?
A SECOND-BY-SECOND SCHEDULE. REAL TIGHT.

WE HAVE A MEETING WITH BIG BELLY BURGER ON POSSIBLE SPONSORSHIP IN FORTY-FIVE MINUTES AND THIRTY-TWO SECONDS.
AND I MUST SAY, AFTER THAT BRILLIANT PERFORMANCE TODAY, IT'S SURE TO BE A LOCK.
SKEETS.

PSHT
I SEE.
SO GETTING ANOTHER PATCH SEWN ON THAT JACKET OF YOURS IS MORE IMPORTANT THAN HELPING PEOPLE LIKE ALAN SCOTT AND ANIMAL MAN?
PEOPLE WHO RISKED THEIR LIVES, WHO MIGHT'VE GIVEN THEM TO SAVE THIS PLANET.

I THOUGHT IT WASN'T ABOUT YOU ANYMORE, BOOSTER.
I THOUGHT YOU WERE FINALLY GETTING YOUR ACT TOGETHER BECAUSE OF TED--

HEY, I DID MY PART, BEA!
I RISKED MY LIFE--
--AND MINE.
--JUMPING BACK HERE FROM THE 25TH CENTURY TO FINISH WHAT TED STARTED.

I HELPED SAVE THE WORLD.
RIP HUNTER-- UNLISTED??
JEFFREY SMITH ?
BONNIE BAXTER ?
S.T.A.R. LABS TIME-TRAVEL DIVISION ?

I HELPED SAVE A FUTURE THAT SPIT IN MY FACE!
SO NOW, YOU KNOW WHAT?!

IT IS ABOUT ME!

SIR?
BIG BELLY BURGER IS WAITING.

I wish the wino would come back.
Day 9 NOTHING
Day 10 NOTHING
Day 11 Wino urinated on door
Day 12 NOTHING
Day 13 NOTHING
READ MY LIPS
Week 4, Day 3

At least that'd be *something*.
Just a little *activity*, anything to break the *monotony* of--

HOW MANY PACKS A DAY?

JEEZ--
OW!

NICE DOODLES.
I *HATE* YOU.
BITE ME.

CAN'T.
NO MOUTH.

YOU DIDN'T ANSWER ME. HOW MANY PACKS A DAY?
WHAT'RE YOU, MY MOTHER?
YOU KNOW, THERE'S CYANIDE GAS IN CIGARETTE SMOKE.
THAT'S THE SAME STUFF THEY USE IN GAS CHAMBERS.
THAT'S VERY MATURE.
I THOUGHT SO.
KEEP UP THE GOOD WORK.
HEY!
WAIT A MINUTE!
YOU SAW MY NOTES, THERE'S NOTHING GOING ON HERE!
NOT YET.
THERE WILL BE, I'M SURE OF IT.
WE'LL TALK AGAIN LATER.
DON'T HOLD YOUR BREATH!
FOUR MORE DAYS, BUDDY! THAT'S IT! FOUR MORE DAYS...
...THEN I'M DONE.

Metropolis.
Steelworks.
DONE WITH IT.
...IT'S THOUGHT THAT SURVIVORS MAY BE TRAPPED INSIDE THE TELEPORTATION BEAM, AND RESCUERS SAY IT COULD STILL BE DAYS BEFORE SCIENTISTS ON THE PLANET RANN...
DON'T YOU UNDERSTAND?
I'M DONE WITH IT, NATASHA.
AND THIS IS ME, SETTING AN EXAMPLE.
THIS IS ME LAYING MY LIFE AS STEEL TO REST.

A WORLD WITHOUT SUPERMAN? I'VE SEEN HOW THAT TURNS OUT.
PEOPLE RUSH IN TO FILL THE VACUUM, BARELY LOOKING AT WHERE THEY'RE GOING.
LIKE I DID.
I'M AFRAID YOU'LL GET HURT, NATASHA.
YOU KNOW IT'S ONE THING... *hrnk*
IT'S ONE THING DOING WHAT'S RIGHT.
IT'S SOMETHING ELSE TO WADE INTO A FIREFIGHT AGAINST A SUPERHUMAN PSYCHOPATH WHO DOESN'T CARE ABOUT YOUR SENSE OF HUMOR OR HOW MUCH YOU LOVE TO WATCH RAINDROPS RUNNING DOWN A WINDOWPANE...
URRR
I DIDN'T EVER WANT TO SET A BAD EXAMPLE OR BE THE WRONG KIND OF INSPIRATION.
I NEVER SHOULD HAVE PUT THAT ARMOR ON...
...SHOULDN'T EVER HAVE STARTED ANY OF THIS.
NOW YOU TELL ME.
YOU REALIZE YOU'RE HALLUCINATING, DON'T YOU, DOC?

HEEEOUAAUR
UCCHH
TDDFF
NATASHA?
NAH.
YOU'RE CHASING YOUR NIECE STRAIGHT OUT OF YOUR LIFE.
BUT YOU CAN'T GET RID OF ME SO EASILY.
UHHH
GAUUHHH
SOMEBODY... DID SOMETHING TO ME...
...POISONED...
YOU GOT THAT RIGHT.
BUT WHO? AND WHY?
I HOPE YOU'RE READY FOR A LONG NIGHT IN HELL, JOHN HENRY.

GGAHHHH
UURRRR
...HAPPENING TO ME... HARNNN...
GUH!
AUUGGHHH!!
MI-001

Week 4, Day 4
YOU DESERVE ANSWERS, MR. DIBNY.
THAT'S WHAT YOU PROMISED TO GIVE ME IF I MET YOU HERE, CASSIE. TIME TO HOLD UP YOUR END OF THE BARGAIN.
WHY DID A CULT OF KRYPTONIAN WORSHIP SCRAWL THE SIGN OF RESURRECTION ON MY WIFE'S GRAVESTONE?
WE DIDN'T. WE'RE NOT VANDALS. WE EXIST TO PREPARE THE WORLD FOR THE RETURN OF A HERO.
YOU SOUND AWFULLY CERTAIN HE'S COMING BACK.
ALL I HAD TO DO WAS TRUST HIS HERITAGE, MR. DIBNY.
THE KRYPTONIANS BELIEVED THAT IMMERSION IN THE STRIPED WATERS OF THE RIVER MEMON GRANTED VISIONS OF THE AFTERLIFE.
DEVEM SHOWED ME. THE WATERS SHOWED ME. I SAW SOMEONE I THOUGHT FOREVER LOST, MR. DIBNY.
DON'T YOU WANT TO SEE?
WHY THE HELL NOT?
ONE THING, SIR. WE WILL NEED TO TAKE SOMETHING IN RETURN.
OH, I GET IT NOW. MONEY--
NO. SOMETHING SIGNIFICANT. WHATEVER IT IS THAT MEANS THE MOST TO YOU.
THEN YOU'RE OUT OF LUCK, KID. ALL THAT EVER MATTERED TO ME WAS SUE. WITH HER GONE, I'VE GOT NOTHING TO OFFER.
SO CUT THE CRAP AND GET THIS SHOW ON THE ROAD. NOW.

HHHUKKK--!
kaff
WHAT THE HELL KIND OF SCAM--?
I DIDN'T SEE ANYTHING! I--
CASSIE?

Week 4, Day 5
It's the rain that does it.
SIMPSOM & Co.
It's like a lullaby...
...like a gentle...
...lullaby...
--Dammit!
Dammitdammitdammit stupidstupidstupid!
Two weeks waiting for something to happen--
--and you almost sleep through it. Good job, Renee, way to earn your money.
Unlocked.
Huh.
So whoever's paying a visit isn't planning on staying long...

Not *hearing* anything.
Not *seeing* anything.

He wasn't more than thirty *seconds* ahead of me, where'd he...

...go.
DON'T EVEN *THINK* ABOUT IT.

HOW'D YOU KNOW IT WAS *ME*?
GUY WHO CAME IN WAS IN *FRONT* OF ME.
YOU'RE THE ONE WHO LIKES TO *SNEAK* UP ON PEOPLE.

TOUCHÉ.
QUESTION IS, WHERE'D HE *GO?*

TAKE A LOOK.

CURIOUS.
HE DIDN'T JUST *VANISH,* THERE'S GOT TO BE A SECRET DOOR OR SOMETHING LIKE THAT.
A SECRET DOOR?

WHAT IS THIS, *D&D?*
GOT A *BETTER* IDEA?
LET'S SEE IF THERE'S STILL *POWER* TO THESE *LIGHTS--*
KLIK

Should've seen *that* coming...
ELF NEEDS FOOD BADLY.
SERIOUSLY, RENEE, YOU NEED TO GET OFF OF ME--
HELL.
...but I think it's fair to say that *this,* not so much.
HNN?
WHAT THE *HELL* IS THAT *THING?!*
HOW SHOULD *I* KNOW?!
KRAK
Fifty pounds of *metal* misses me by inches.
YOU WANTED ME TO *WATCH* THIS PLACE!
I FIGURED *YOU* KNEW WHAT WAS GOING *ON!*

Two double-taps, four bullets, all good *hits...*

BLAM

hnff!

...doesn't even *slow* the thing *down.*

It's on top of me in a *blur,* I barely get my *pistol* up--

--I land on something cold, something sharp--

--for a moment I don't know *who* I am--

--why I'm *here...*

nff

WHOOM

...vision comes back in time for me to see things go from bad to worse...
RRGGNN
...and then I see guns all around me, weapons like I've never seen before...
NRRAAAR!!!
BUT HOW DO YOU REALLY FEEL?
GGRRRR--
--HNNNR?
DAMN.

Week 4, Day 7
THIS IS OPERATION LIGHTNING STRIKE!
WE'VE SPOKEN WITH THE RANNIANS AND HALO THINKS SHE CAN INFLUENCE THE ZETA CURRENT TO GROUND ITSELF IN WESTERN AUSTRALIA.
THIS IS IT, FOLKS.
WUMMMMMMMMMMMMM
ZETA BEAM IMPACT IN THE NORTHERN TERRITORY OF AUSTRALIA.
LET'S BRING THOSE HEROES HOME!
DID WE GET THEM?
TELL ME WE GOT THEM.
TELL ME THEY'RE OKAY... oh...

NEXT IN 52

WEEK FOUR NOTES

GREG RUCKA

There are so many things about this issue to remark upon, and no particular way for me to cull the comments. This was the first issue to focus in large part on the Montoya/Question storyline, and the first time those two characters truly got to interact in any substantial way, so for that reason alone it's a personal favorite. I think it was this issue, in fact, that had editor Steve Wacker calling them the "Maddie and Dave" of the DCU. For those of you who don't get the reference, watch a couple of first season episodes of *Moonlighting* and all will become clear.

One of the lovely things about this week, for me, was how beautifully the collaboration worked on every level. What the writers brought was augmented by Keith's layouts and then finished to a fine gloss with Joe Bennett's art. Little touches of elegance pepper the whole issue.

I'm looking at page 1, the Montoya P.I. trope narrative, half Raymond Chandler, half Douglas Adams, and the private eye writer in me is screaming "but down these mean streets a man must go who is not himself mean, who is neither tarnished nor afraid." And damn if that wasn't Vic Sage's journey, and later if it wouldn't be Renee Montoya's. And damn if those streets don't actually look *mean*. That's Joe, he brought that, and Jack Jadson's inks highlighted it, and Alex Sinclair's colors sold it.

First page of the issue, bottom left-hand panel — see how Montoya is actually *chewing* the aspirin she's taking? It's a wonderful bit of characterization, and it's all Keith; he put a note in the breakdowns — "dry crunches/chews aspirin (old drunk's trick to quicken relief)".

(It's taking a lot of energy on my part not to go for the cheap shot at Giffen's expense here, for the record. You know, something like, "Hmm, and he would know." Oh, look. There, I did it anyway. Heh.)

And now the second page. "Lightning that can't strike." That's Grant. That's pure, beautiful Grant. Such a powerful, spooky, elegant image, and in its own way it meshes seamlessly with the John Henry delirium later in the issue, which was thoroughly terrifying in its own right — all the more so because the reader truly has no clue whatsoever what's going on with him.

Just a wonderful marriage of tone, dovetailing perfectly with the Ralph sequence. In fact, the whole issue has a mystery novel feel to it, and rereading it now, I'm wondering how consciously we were pursuing that — from the first-person P.I. narrative to the unreliable narrator that's John Henry and the inexplicable behavior of Booster Gold, threading back to the series' other detective, Ralph Dibny, pursuing his own investigation. Like Montoya, the mystery gives Ralph purpose, rouses him to action. Thematically, their stories follow similar trajectories, ending in very different places at year's end; both find themselves grappling with grief as much as with death, trying to find some sense of meaning in the losses each of them endures.

MARK WAID

The Question/Montoya scene here, all Greg, is one of the high points of the entire series. Their relationship is like no other in the story.

BREAKDOWNS

BY **KEITH GIFFEN**

Ralph is submerged in Kryptonian waters, hoping to get a glimpse of the afterlife and his dead wife Sue. Only . . . nothing. Compare with page 89.

Week 5, Day 1

LCOME HOME HERO

DAD'S NOT *COMING* HOME FROM SPACE, IS HE?

DC COMICS 52

WRITTEN BY GEOFF JOHNS, GRANT MORRISON, GREG RUCKA, MARK WAID

ART BREAKDOWNS BY KEITH GIFFEN • PENCILS BY CHRIS BATISTA
INKS BY JIMMY PALMIOTTI • COLORS BY ALEX SINCLAIR

LETTERING BY PHIL BALSMAN • COVER BY JG JONES & ALEX SINCLAIR
ASSISTANT EDITORS JANN JONES & HARVEY RICHARDS • EDITED BY STEPHEN WACKER

ALAN SCOTT.
GREEN LANTERN.

I WONDERED WHEN ONE OF YOU GUYS WOULD SHOW UP.
IS THIS ABOUT MY HUSBAND?
I'M SO SORRY.
ANIMAL MAN WENT MISSING IN ACTION OUT IN SPACE.
HIS BRAVERY WAS EXCEPTIONAL.

YEAH.
THAT SOUNDS LIKE BUDDY.
"MISSING," HUH?

SO THERE'S STILL HOPE.

Week 5
STARS IN THEIR COURSES

...WGBS BRINGING YOU THIS SPECIAL ANNOUNCEMENT...
DAILY PLANET

IN WHAT HE'S DESCRIBED AS "THE SINGLE MOST SIGNIFICANT DEVELOPMENT IN EVOLUTION SINCE FISH CRAWLED OUT OF THE SEA..."
ANYTHING YOU FORGOT TO TELL ME, PARTNER?

LEX LUTHOR CLAIMS TO HAVE SYNTHESIZED HUMAN VARIANT METAGENE, THE BIOLOGICAL QUIRK THAT ALLOWS FOR SO-CALLED "SUPERPOWERS..."
DAILY PLANET

I WANT TO REDEEM MYSELF, IN A WAY, YES.

AND I'D LIKE TO BE VERY CLEAR ABOUT WHAT THIS MEANS.

IT MEANS WE NO LONGER HAVE TO TRUST OUR SAFETY TO THE PRIVILEGED ELITE, THE ACCIDENTAL FEW.

IT MEANS EVERY MAN AND WOMAN CAN BE A SUPERHERO.

SUPERMAN IS GONE, BUT HERE'S THE GOOD NEWS.
WE NO LONGER NEED HIM OR ANY OF HIS KIND.
THE AGE OF THE SUPER-CITIZEN IS DAWNING.
PAGING DOCTOR IRONS.
PAGING DOCTOR IRONS.
THIS IS STEEL.
I'M ON MY WAY.
"WELCOME TO SAINT CAMILLUS..."
EMERGENCY

WAS...WAS THAT HAWKGIRL OUTSIDE?
SHE WAS 25 FEET TALL...
ALAN SCOTT. I BELIEVE WE'VE MET ONCE OR TWICE.
WE APPRECIATE THE RAPID RESPONSE, DOCTOR IRONS.
WE'VE BEEN CALLING EVERYONE.

I'M JOHN, ALAN.
THIS PLACE IS INCREDIBLE.
JOHN, THIS IS DOCTOR PIETER CROSS A.K.A. DOCTOR MID-NITE.
PIETER'S A SPECIALIST IN METAHUMAN MEDICAL CARE...
WORKING WITH THE JSA, I'VE HAD TO BE.
A PLEASURE, DOCTOR IRONS.

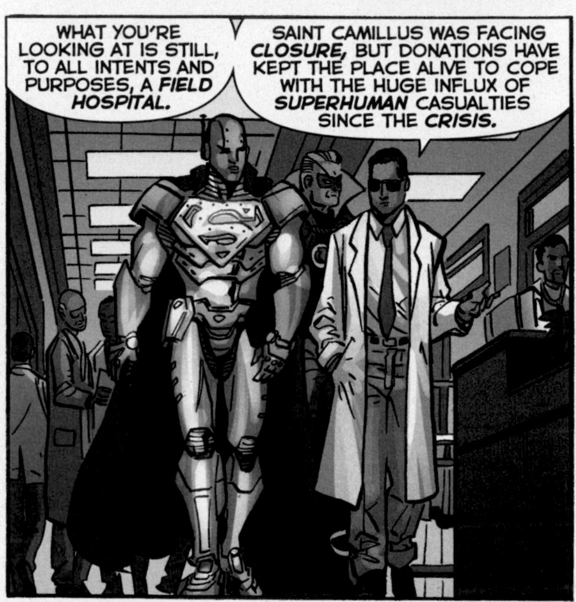
WHAT YOU'RE LOOKING AT IS STILL, TO ALL INTENTS AND PURPOSES, A FIELD HOSPITAL.
SAINT CAMILLUS WAS FACING CLOSURE, BUT DONATIONS HAVE KEPT THE PLACE ALIVE TO COPE WITH THE HUGE INFLUX OF SUPERHUMAN CASUALTIES SINCE THE CRISIS.

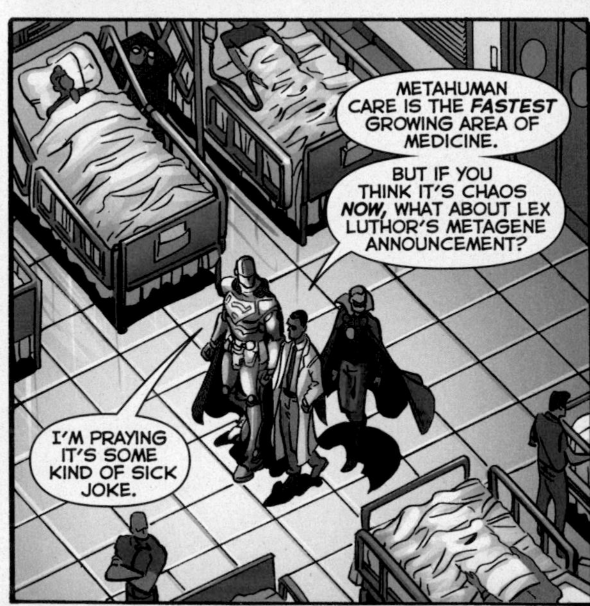
METAHUMAN CARE IS THE FASTEST GROWING AREA OF MEDICINE.
BUT IF YOU THINK IT'S CHAOS NOW, WHAT ABOUT LEX LUTHOR'S METAGENE ANNOUNCEMENT?
I'M PRAYING IT'S SOME KIND OF SICK JOKE.

DOES ANYONE HONESTLY BELIEVE HE'S REFORMED?
CAN I ASK WHAT HAPPENED TO HAWKGIRL?

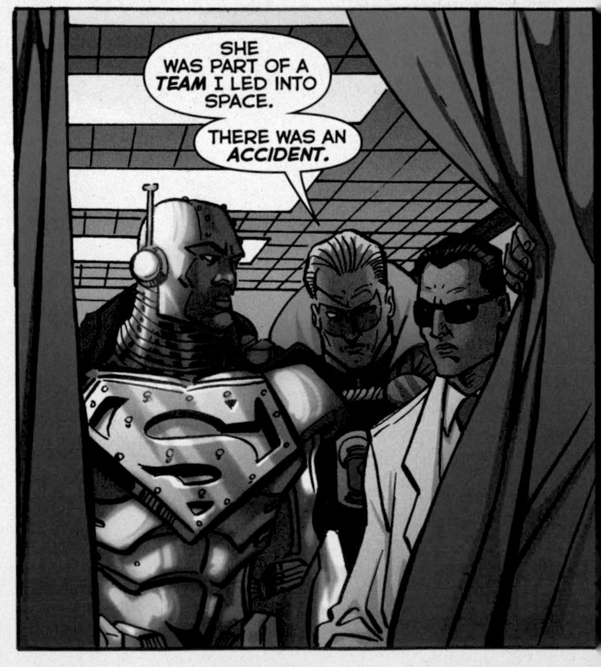
SHE WAS PART OF A TEAM I LED INTO SPACE.
THERE WAS AN ACCIDENT.

A TELEPORTATION ACCIDENT?
OH MY GOD.
MOLECULAR FUSION.
I HAVE CYBORG AND FIRESTORM ON ONE OF THE NEW TIME-FREEZING DRUGS WHILE WE TRY TO FIGURE OUT HOW TO SEPARATE THEIR NERVOUS SYSTEMS.

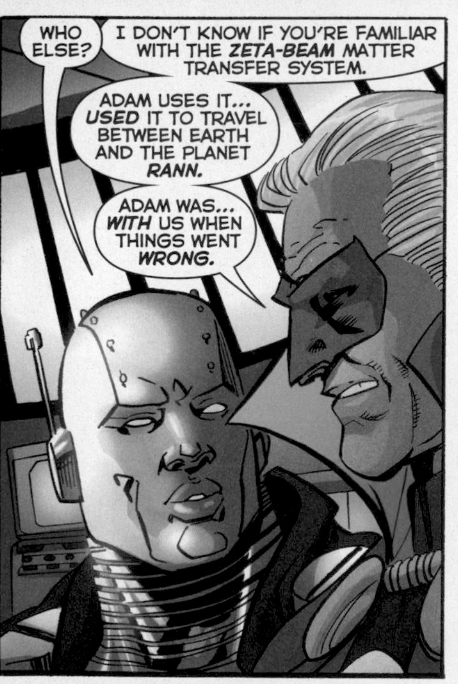

WHO ELSE?
I DON'T KNOW IF YOU'RE FAMILIAR WITH THE ZETA-BEAM MATTER TRANSFER SYSTEM.
ADAM USES IT... USED IT TO TRAVEL BETWEEN EARTH AND THE PLANET RANN.
ADAM WAS... WITH US WHEN THINGS WENT WRONG.

HE DID WHAT HE COULD... EVERYONE DID THEIR VERY BEST.
BUT HE DIDN'T MAKE IT BACK.

THE ZETA BEAM WAS... REFRACTED... I DON'T REALLY KNOW WHAT HAPPENED.
BUT PEOPLE WERE BADLY HURT.
HOW CAN I HELP?
THIS YOUNG MAN IS ONE OF THE TITANS, RIGHT?

WHAT WAS HE DOING OUT IN *SPACE?*
WHOSE IDEA WAS *THAT?* HE BARELY HAS *POWERS* FROM WHAT I KNOW.
WHAT IS *THAT* THING?
MAL DUNCAN.
THE AH...*SPEAKER* APPARATUS HAS BEEN IDENTIFIED AS BELONGING TO THE *RED TORNADO* ANDROID.
HIS BODY'S *REJECTING* THE FUSION BUT WE CAN'T *OPERATE* WITHOUT REMOVING HIS *LUNGS...*
UNFORTUNATELY HE'S DEVELOPED A SEVERE *CHEST* INFECTION AND ACUTE *SEPTICEMIA.*

THE ZETA BEAM SHOULD BE INSTANTANEOUS, RIGHT?
SO WHERE WERE YOU BETWEEN BEING THERE A MONTH AGO AND ARRIVING HERE LAST WEEK?
THAT'S THE BIG QUESTION, ISN'T IT?
YOU'VE BEEN ON SPACE MISSIONS, JOHN... IT ALL HAPPENS SO FAST, WITH NO UP AND NO DOWN AND...NO SOUND.
THERE'S NO SOUND IN SPACE.
I LOST AN EYE.
AND IT TURNS OUT THE ONE I DO HAVE ISN'T EVEN MY OWN...
BUT, WHATEVER HAPPENED... I GOT OFF LIGHT.
PSEUDOCYTES WILL SELF-REPLICATE AND SHUT DOWN THE PARTS OF HIS IMMUNE RESPONSE THAT ARE CAUSING MAN/MACHINE GRAFT REJECTION...
THEY'LL WORK AS AN ARTIFICIAL IMMUNE SYSTEM UNTIL HIS OWN RECOVERS.
BUT WE MAY NEED TO CHARGE THEM.
THERE WAS NO SOUND.
BUT WE HAD TELEPATHIC CONTACT.

"THE AFTEREFFECTS OF HEALING A RIFT IN SPACE OVER NINETY-FIVE MILLION MILES WIDE WERE UNBELIEVABLE.
"IT WASN'T JUST ENERGY THAT EMANATED FROM IT.
"IT WAS SOME KIND OF REALITY-WARPING WAVE.
"I WATCHED SHIPS REVERT TO THE RAW METALS THEY WERE MADE OF. I SAW KHUNDS EVOLVE MILLIONS OF YEARS INTO BEINGS OF PURE MENTAL ENERGY.
"TIME WOULD SPEED UP, THEN REWIND.
"I'M NOT SURE HOW MANY TIMES I LIVED THROUGH IT.

"ADAM STRANGE TOLD MAL DUNCAN TO OPEN UP A PORTAL THAT WOULD LEAD TO THE NORTHERN HEMISPHERE OF THE PLANET RANN--
"--ALL IN HOPES OF REDIVERTING A ZETA BEAM TO OUR LOCATION IN ORDER TO TELEPORT US BACK TO EARTH.
"A MOMENT LATER--
"--THE ZETA BEAM CAME THROUGH.
"BUT SOMETHING WENT WRONG. IT WAS SPLINTERED BY THE PORTAL, LIKE A RAY OF LIGHT SENT THROUGH A PRISM.
"A BEAM STRUCK CYBORG AND FIRESTORM, FUSING THEM TOGETHER.
"ANOTHER HIT HAWKGIRL AND BUMBLEBEE.
"STILL ANOTHER SENT SUPERGIRL... SOMEWHERE.
"MAL DUNCAN'S BLOOD FROZE IN THE VACUUM OF SPACE AS RED TORNADO EXPLODED.
"THERE WAS SHRAPNEL.
"AND THEN DARKNESS JOINED THE SILENCE.
"UNTIL THE SCREAMS OF EVERYONE FILLED MY MIND.
"UNTIL WE FINALLY ARRIVED HOME."

LANTERN?
I'M FINE.

A MAN SHOULDN'T HAVE TO MOURN HIS OWN CHILDREN, SHOULD HE?
WE SHOULDN'T HAVE TO BURY OUR CHILDREN.

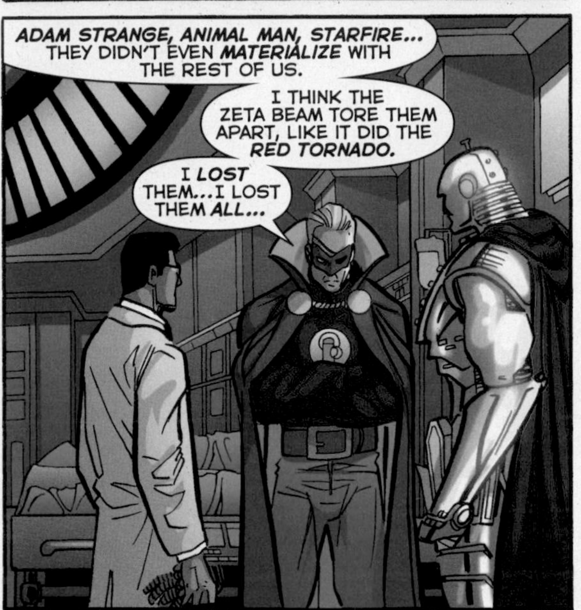
ADAM STRANGE, ANIMAL MAN, STARFIRE... THEY DIDN'T EVEN MATERIALIZE WITH THE REST OF US.
I THINK THE ZETA BEAM TORE THEM APART, LIKE IT DID THE RED TORNADO.
I LOST THEM...I LOST THEM ALL...

YOU KNOW, I KEEP THINKING HOW I'VE LIVED A HUNDRED LIVES IN THIS ONE.
AND I THINK OF ALL THOSE BRAVE YOUNG FACES.
I'D GIVE MY LIFE RIGHT NOW IF IT COULD BRING EVEN ONE OF THEM BACK.

SORRY, DOC.
I DON'T USUALLY MAKE A FOOL OF MYSELF LIKE THIS.
BUT MY DAUGHTER... JADE... SHE DIDN'T MAKE IT BACK EITHER.

NURSE!

I DON'T LIKE THE SOUND OF THIS YOUNG MAN'S BREATHING...

IT'S NOT JUST THE PHYSICAL TRAUMA.
THESE PEOPLE ARE GOING TO NEED COUNSELLING.
YOU TOO, ALAN.
COUNSELLING?
JOHN, I WAS ONE OF THE FIRST TO ACCEPT THE RESPONSIBILITY OF PROTECTING THE EARTH, ALL THOSE YEARS AGO.

IT'S MY JOB TO SET AN EXAMPLE.
I HAVE TO SHOW WE DON'T BREAK LIKE OTHER PEOPLE.
WE DON'T GIVE IN TO FATE.

HE'S IN ARREST!
CRASH TEAM!

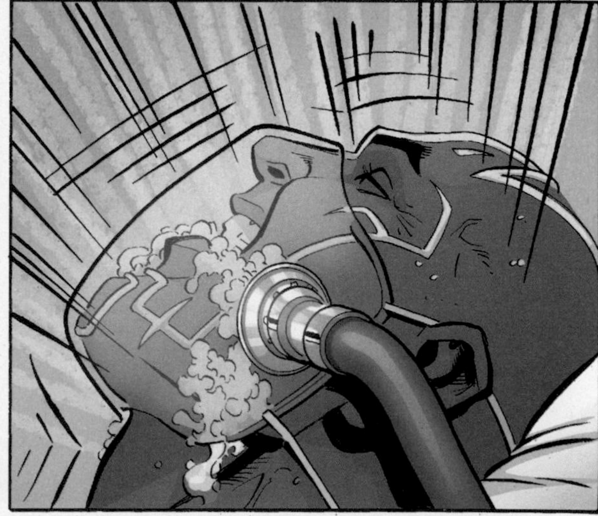

Gotham City.
...THEIR RETURN, BUT THERE'S, LIKE, NO RELIABLE INFORMATION...

C'MON, RENEE, I CAN HEAR THE $*@$ING TELEVISION, OKAY? I KNOW YOU'RE HOME!
GIVE A GIRL A BREAK, CAPTAIN. I'M DOING EVERYTHING WITH ONLY ONE WORKING ARM RIGHT NOW.
...HAWKGIRL OVER TWENTY-FIVE FEET TALL! THAT WOULD MAKE HER WINGSPAN ABOUT WHAT, TED?

IT'S LIKE A SAUNA IN HERE.
YEAH, THE A.C.'S DEAD.
YOU WANT A BEER?
SURE.
PRETTY DAMN BIG, I'D IMAGINE, LENNY.

HELP YOURSELF. IF YOU'RE DRINKING, THAT MEANS YOU'RE OFF THE CLOCK.
FIGURED I'D GET FURTHER WITH YOU THAT WAY.
I'LL TELL TOBY YOU SAID THAT.

YOU KNOW WHY I'M HERE, RENEE.
YEP.
YOU GONNA TELL ME WHAT HAPPENED?

I ALREADY TOLD YOU EVERYTHING I COULD, MAGGIE.
RIGHT. WAREHOUSE WITH TRICK BASEMENT FULL OF FANCY GUNS. MONSTER ATTACKS YOU. YOU VAPORIZE MONSTER.
QUICK VERSION, BUT YEAH.

THE PLACE IS CLEAN, RENEE.
THE ONLY PROOF I'VE GOT THIS HAPPENED AT ALL IS YOUR MULTIPLE FRACTURES, THAT'S IT.

I TOLD YOU EVERYTHING I COULD.

YOU DIDN'T TELL ME WHO HIRED YOU.

YOU'RE NOT LICENSED, RENEE. YOU'RE NOT A P.I., YOU DON'T GET THEIR PRIVILEGES OF CONFIDENTIALITY.
MAYBE I SHOULD FIX THAT.
CAN I COUNT ON YOU FOR A RECOMMENDATION TO THE LICENSING BOARD?

YOU CAN COUNT ON ME BRINGING THE HAMMER DOWN, HARD, IF THIS HAPPENS AGAIN.
I'VE ONLY GOT YOUR WORD THAT ANYTHING HAPPENED ON KANE STREET AT ALL.
YOU THINK THE BROKEN ARM IS FOR SHOW?

NO, I BELIEVE EVERY-THING YOU'VE SAID HAPPENED DID HAPPEN.

WHICH MEANS YOU'RE INTO SOMETHING VERY BIG AND VERY BAD BUT YOU WON'T GIVE ME THE PROOF I NEED TO HELP YOU.
I DON'T NEED HELP.
I HOPE YOU'RE RIGHT, BECAUSE I SURE AS HELL DON'T WANT TO SEE YOUR NAME ON THE BOARD IN RED.

YOU TAKE CARE OF YOURSELF, RENEE.

DON'T WORRY ABOUT THAT.

HUFF
HUFF
WE'RE LOSING HIM!
DAMMIT!
WHERE'S MY TEAM!?
GIVE IN TO FATE?
NEVER.
STAND BACK, PLEASE.

ZZZZAAAP
HHUJIII
IT'S COMING!

EMERGENCY

52!
52!

UHHHH

OWW.
WHAT WAS THAT, SOME KIND OF PLAYBACK?
THE RED TORNADO'S LAST WORDS.

WHAT WAS HE TALKING ABOUT?
WHAT'S COMING?

"WHAT DID HE *SEE?*"

D'YOU THINK THEY *WON?*

BACK HOME, I MEAN.

IS THE CRISIS *OVER?*

DID WE SAVE THE EARTH?

WILL THEY SEND OUT A SEARCH PARTY?

YOU KNOW, WHAT IF MY WIFE AND KIDS THINK I'M *DEAD* AND THROW OUT MY *STUFF?*

ONLY AN EARTHMAN COULD LOOK SO UNCOMFORTABLE IN *PARADISE.*

WE *SURVIVED.*

WE EVEN CRASH-LANDED IN *HEAVEN*--CAN'T YOU MAKE THE *BEST* OF IT, BUDDY BAKER?

THE TALES OF TAMARAN'S STARFARERS SPEAK OF A LONG-LOST PERFECT PLANET LIKE THIS.
IT COMES FROM A MUCH GRANDER UNIVERSE AND VISITS OUR OWN ONCE IN EVERY GENERATION.

ACCORDING TO MY NANNY.
IT'S OKAY FOR YOU.
YOU GUYS LIVE IN SPACE.

THIS IS THE FIRST TIME I'VE BEEN MAROONED ON AN ALIEN PLANET AND IT'S KINDA FREAKING ME OUT.

HAVE YOU NOTICED THE SUN'S BEEN SETTING FOR ABOUT TWO WEEKS NOW?
I'M NOT USED TO THAT.
AND I'VE HAD MY FAIR SHARE OF WEIRD EXPERIENCES AS ANIMAL MAN BUT I'VE NEVER BEEN THIS FAR AWAY FROM HOME.

YOU DON'T EVEN KNOW HOW FAR.
EARTH MUST BE COUNTLESS LIGHT-YEARS FROM HERE.
LIGHT-CENTURIES EVEN.

UNTIL THEN WE HAVE ABSOLUTELY NO IDEA WHERE THE ZETA BEAM HAS DUMPED US.
AND IF THE APTLY NAMED ADAM STRANGE DOESN'T COME THROUGH, WE MAY BE HERE FOR QUITE SOME TIME.
I HEARD THAT.
I GOT US INTO THIS AND I PROMISED I'D GET US OUT OF IT, DIDN'T I?
NONE OF THAT'S CHANGED, PRINCESS.

EYES OR NO EYES.

IF YOU THINK YOU CAN FONDLE THAT SPACESHIP BACK TO LIFE, BE MY GUEST.
ALL I'M SAYING IS, I'VE BEEN USING MY SUPERSENSES TO PROBE THE PLANET'S MORPHIC FIELD NETWORK.
AND GUESS WHAT?

THERE'S A SERPENT IN PARADISE, GUYS.
I'M NOT TRYING TO ALARM ANYBODY, BUT I HAVE A FEELING WE SHOULD GET OFF THIS PLANET BEFORE THE SUN GOES DOWN.

BECAUSE WE'RE NOT ALONE.
NEXT IN
IS ALL HIS FAULT
IS ALL HIS

WEEK FIVE NOTES

MARK WAID

Week Five marked the writing team's first real procedural departure. For our first four issues, the working process was standard: editor Steve Wacker would assemble the writers on an international conference call; we'd discuss the notes we'd made in our in-person meetings, developing sentence fragments like "Montoya reveals she stole a weapon from the warehouse" into full scenes; we'd plot all twenty pages as a group; and then we'd divide sequences and pages into individual assignments and scurry off to our keyboards to type. Often, particularly at first, the division of labor was more time consuming than was the plotting and sounded like a big, rapid-fire game of Pit played across transatlantic phone lines:

Me: "Greg, how many pages do you need for that Montoya scene? It says 'six' in our notes, but can you squeeze it into five so I can turn this Booster scene into a two-page spread?"

Greg: "I think so...yeah, yeah...but I was going to ask for an extra page for the Steel beat because he hasn't met Luthor yet and that has to happen before the month is over."

Geoff: "Guys, don't forget we have to show Black Adam this issue, too. Would it help if I just had him in the background, on a TV screen in Magnus's lab or something?"

Me: "Perfect. Also, I can move the Ralph beat to next issue, but to account for his seven-day absence, I'll need four pages instead of two."

Grant: "[something in a barely intelligible Scottish accent] space heroes [Scottish, Scottish] Styx, yeah."

Me, Geoff, Greg, Steve: "Come again?"

Week Five broke the "all in" format. It was a whole lotta Grant and a little Greg that week because I was at an overseas convention and Geoff, like everyone else in comics, was busy inking pages of INFINITE CRISIS #7. Yes, we'd broken out the basic beats of the script as a team, but the first I read a single word of it as an actual manuscript was in an airport in Sydney, Australia. I genuinely missed not having pages in this issue, but the surprise tradeoff was in getting the unforeseen opportunity to experience Week Five the same as the audience — having no certainty of what was coming because I'd typed none of it. For the first time, I saw the bigger picture of 52 — and, more important, I saw that it was going to work.

Some specific comments:

Yes, we all know how stupid it is to have a hero who wears both a mask AND an eyepatch. Not our fault. I suggested we add a big, green parrot on his shoulder, too, but no one listened.

Saint Camillus, the hospital for super-humans, was 52's first big new addition to the DC Universe. My memory is that we spent a crazy amount of time coming up with the name and that Greg coined it after the patron saint of caregivers. Either that, or he pulled it off a gin bottle.

The Space Heroes make their first appearance. Initially, we were given a pool of four spacesters we could choose our three from — meaning that our blind guide could very well have been Captain Comet — but, ultimately, we decided that having two guys stuck roaming the stars with a naked Starfire allowed for more tension if both men were happily married.

(COMPARE WITH PAGE 116 OF THIS COLLECTION)

52 WEEK FIVE — PAGE EIGHTEEN

PANEL ONE
Space — the curved rim of a planetary horizon. We're among a shower of meteors that burns as they hit the atmosphere, leading our eye down towards a lovely heart-shaped continent set in a sparkling sea with temperate weather systems swirling.

PANEL TWO
Move in on the planet's surface. It's like some EC Comics Eden by Wally Wood — a lush and perfect garden world in the light of a pure radiant sun. This world is Adon, first seen in the final issue of FOREVER PEOPLE — a ruined ship crashed and overgrown in this glorious landscape.

PANEL THREE
Buddy Baker, Animal Man, looking up at the liquid stars in the twilight skies of Adon. He sits on a coralline rock formation which juts into a sparkling rock pool fed by waterfalls. Huge overhanging swaths of colorful fruit and flowers overhang the pool. It all looks perfect. Animal Man's costume hangs drying on a bough beside Starfire's costume. It's torn in places. He's wearing his faithful jacket — battered, scuffed and ragged in places, and a pair of briefs.

BUDDY: Do you think they WON?

BUDDY: Back home, I mean.

PANEL FOUR
Close on Buddy looking up at the stars. He holds a photo of his family in his hand and it's been burned at the edges.

BUDDY: Is the Crisis OVER?

BUDDY: Did we save Earth?

BUDDY: Will they send out a search party?

PANEL FIVE
Now Starfire rises from the pool in foreground, gloriously naked and running her hands through her luxurious hair. Buddy turns to look at her, not at all startled by her nakedness.

BUDDY: What if my wife and kids think I'm DEAD and throw out my STUFF?

STARFIRE: Only an Earthman could look so uncomfortable in PARADISE.

STARFIRE: We SURVIVED. We even crash-landed in HEAVEN — can't you make the BEST of it, Buddy Baker?

...LIVE FROM THE MIDTOWN TRAIN STATION, WHERE FORMER JUSTICE LEAGUE MEMBER BOOSTER GOLD JUST SAVED THOUSANDS OF METROPOLIS CITIZENS FROM AN ARMORED MARAUDER.
I UNDERSTAND WE HAVE AMATEUR CAM-PHONE VIDEO OF THIS VILLAIN'S STRUGGLE TO BOMB THE CITY'S BUSIEST SUBWAY PLATFORM...
MANTHRAX
POLICE DO NOT CROSS
WMET-TV LIVE
CAM-PHONE FOOTAGE
CURSE YOU, BOOSTER GOLD!
"CURSE YOU, BOOSTER GOLD"?
I AD-LIBBED. THAT'S WHAT ACTORS DO.
WMET-TV LIVE
I TEACH A SATURDAY MORNING IMPROV AT THE LEARNING ANNEX. YOU SHOULD STOP BY.
THIS SATURDAY? LOVE TO.
REALLY?
ABSOLUTELY. WE CAN MAKE BROWNIES AFTER. MAYBE BRAID EACH OTHER'S HAIR.
Week 6, Day 1
DC COMICS 52
WRITTEN BY GEOFF JOHNS, GRANT MORRISON, GREG RUCKA, MARK WAID

WITH US NOW WE HAVE **SKEETS,** BOOSTER GOLD'S **ROBOTIC SIDEKICK.** SKEETS, FILL US **IN.**

I'M TOLD BOOSTER RATHER ABRUPTLY STORMED OUT OF A CRUCIAL **ENDORSEMENT MEETING** WITH **PROMETHIUM RAZORS** WHEN HE HEARD ABOUT THIS CRISIS. WILL THAT SOUR THEIR **NEGOTIATION?**

WE HOPE NOT, MS. LANPHER, BUT PRIORITIES ARE PRIORITIES. THE THINGS BOOSTER DOES AREN'T ABOUT DOLLAR FIGURES.

OR, ***ALTERNATIVELY,*** BOB--

BILL.

--***BILL***--YOU CAN GO FIND A HORSE TO CHOKE WITH THE MONEY YOU JUST MADE, THEN VANISH INTO THE SAME OBSCURE TALENT AGENCY WHERE I FOUND YOU.

ART BREAKDOWNS BY KEITH GIFFEN PENCILS BY JOE BENNETT INKS BY RUY JOSE
COLORS BY ALEX SINCLAIR LETTERING BY NICK J. NAPOLITANO

...AND, ONCE **DISARMED,** THE HELPLESS VILLAIN VANISHED INTO THE SUBWAY **TUNNELS** AS BOOSTER CALMED **PANICKED BYSTANDERS.** SKEETS, WILL MANTHRAX BE BROUGHT TO **JUSTICE?**
IF THIS MISCREANT EVER SHOWS HIS MASK IN METROPOLIS ***AGAIN,*** HE'LL HAVE TO ANSWER TO ***BOOSTER GOLD!***
YOU MAY ***QUOTE*** ME!

I'LL TAKE THE ***HELMET.***
DROP THE ***SUIT*** AT THE SAME STORAGE LOCKER YOU PICKED IT ***UP*** FROM, MANTHRAX DISAPPEARS ***FOREVER*** AS SUDDENLY AS HE APPEARED, WE NEVER HAD THIS ***CONVERSATION,*** EVERYONE ***WINS.***
CAPISCE.

COVER BY J.G. JONES & ALEX SINCLAIR
ASSISTANT EDITORS JANN JONES & HARVEY RICHARDS
EDITED BY STEPHEN WACKER
AND BECAUSE I'M A GENEROUS SOUL, I'LL GIVE YOU SOME ADVICE:
I'D TURN THAT DOUGH INTO PROMETHIUM RAZORS STOCK BEFORE THE MARKETS CLOSE TODAY.
COAST CLEAR ABOVE, SKEETS?
AFFIRMATIVE, SIR! PROMETHIUM WISHES TO RESCHEDULE. I TOLD THEM TOMORROW.
THIS AFTERNOON, WE TRAVEL TO ARIZONA. I FINALLY LOCATED A LAST KNOWN ADDRESS, AS YOU REQUESTED, FOR DR. RIP HUNTER.
THEN WE'RE OFF. DON'T SPEND THAT ALL IN ONE PLACE, BOB.
I'M NOT SURE I COULD.
BURGER
BEER
CHINA SYNDROME
WEEK 6

<YOU ARE VIOLATING CHINESE AIRSPACE, GREEN LANTERNS.>
<YOU HAVE IGNORED THE REQUESTS OF THE CHINESE GOVERNMENT TO RETREAT.>
<*AUGUST GENERAL IN IRON* TO GREAT WALL. REQUESTING COALITION SUPPORT.>
WHO THE HELL ARE THEY, JORDAN?

I THINK THEY'RE *GOOD GUYS,* JOHN.

<WHEN ARE WE TO JOIN THE OTHERS?>
<THE GREAT TEN WERE GATHERED TO CONSOLIDATE SUPERHUMAN POWER FOR THE PRESERVATION OF CHINA--
--AND YET WE SPEND MOST OF OUR DAY WAITING FOR THE GREEN LIGHT TO FLASH. BUREAUCRACY WILL BE THE DEATH OF US, PERFECT PHYSICIAN.>
<MOTHER OF CHAMPIONS IS STILL HOURS AWAY FROM GIVING BIRTH TO OUR NEXT ARMY OF SUPERMEN.>
<WE HAVE NO TIME TO WAIT FOR HER NEWBORN CANNON FODDER. THE LACK OF CONTROL OVER THE AMERICANS THREATENS EVEN THE GHOST FOX WOMEN OF MY FAR-AWAY HOMELAND.>
<JUST LET ME KILL THESE TWO AND ADD THEM TO MY LEGION OF SPIRITS!>
<AUGUST GENERAL SHOULD APPROVE THAT AS SOON AS I FINISH FILING OUR REPORTS ON OUR RECENT CONFRONTATION WITH THE SUPER YOUNG TEAM.>
<FLAMBOYANT FOOLS. THEY NEARLY LET BRIMSTONE DESTROY TOKYO. IF IT WERE NOT FOR THE SOLAR POWERS OF THE SOCIALIST RED GUARDSMAN-->
<AUGUST GENERAL IN IRON TO GREAT TEN. PERMISSION FOR RELEASE WAS DENIED (THE IDIOTS).>
<COALITION SUPPORT HAS BEEN APPROVED AND IS ON THE WAY.>

<IMMORTAL-MAN-IN-DARKNESS TO AUGUST GENERAL IN IRON. I HAVE **GREEN LANTERN POINT ONE** IN MY SIGHTS.>
<REQUESTING PERMISSION PER CODEX **SIX-SIX-THREE** TO TAKE HIM OUT OF THE SKY.>
<CODEX **SIX-SIX-THREE** CLEARED. PERMISSION GRANTED.>
HOPE YOU'RE WEARING A PARACHUTE.
<I DO NOT NEED ONE.>
BOOOOMM

FWMPP
BWWOOSH

OM MANI PADME HUM
WHAT DOES THAT--?
ALL HAIL THE JEWEL IN THE LOTUS.

IT IS MY HOLIEST OF PRAYERS. IT ALLOWS ME ACCESS TO THE BUDDHIST SIDDHIS.
--ARRRGHH!
I AM THUNDER-MIND.
WHAT ARE YOUR INTENTIONS?
W-WE'RE JUST HERE FOR EVIL STAR. HE'S INVOLVED IN EXTRATERRESTRIAL WEAPONS TRADING.

AS A REPRESENTATIVE OF THE GREEN LANTERN CORPS, IT'S MY JOB TO REIN IN ALL ALIEN ACTIVITY THAT THREATENS--
-ARRHH!
THIS IS OUR COUNTRY, GREEN LANTERN.
YOU WILL LEAVE EVIL STAR TO US.

NO CAN DO, BUDDHA.
THIS IS EARTH'S PROBLEM.
WHAM

THESE MORONS ARE SO LUCKY I DON'T HAVE ACCESS TO ANY OF MY DEVICES.
I HAVEN'T BEEN SO ANGRY FOR A LONG TIME.
CAN YOU BELIEVE WHAT THEY DID ? THEY TOOK MY RESEARCH, WILL.
THE PINBOARD WITH THE MISSING SCIENTISTS! THE ENTIRE DOSSIER.
EVERYTHING. THE LOT.
AND YOU KNOW WHY?
NOT BECAUSE I'D STUMBLED ONTO SOME BIG GOVERNMENT COVER-UP, OH NO! NOTHING LIKE THAT.
IT'S BECAUSE I CONVERTED ONE OF THE GUARDS' I-PODS INTO A HAND HELD SONIC DISINTEGRATOR RAY AND SOMEBODY DIDN'T LIKE IT.
CAN I HELP THE WAY MY MIND WORKS?
I'LL BE A HERO TO THE MACHINE PEOPLE OF THE FUTURE! WHY CAN'T I GET SOME RESPECT IN THE HERE AND NOW.
I DON'T KNOW.
MAYBE IT'S YOUR WILLINGNESS TO KILL PEOPLE IF THEY GET IN YOUR WAY, PROFESSOR MORROW.
YOU SHOULD TRY THE BOOK ON MEDITATION I BROUGHT. IT REALLY HELPED ME AFTER EVERYTHING WENT WRONG WITH MY METAL MEN AND ALL THAT OTHER STUFF.

NO MORE TROUBLE FROM YOU, MORROW.
WE'RE WATCHING YOU.
THANKS FOR YOUR PATIENCE, DOCTOR MAGNUS.
HMM.
OTHER MEN WATCH THE PLAYBOY CHANNEL BUT YOU WATCH ME.
WHICH OF US IS PUNISHED MORE, I WONDER?
UM...AFTER OUR LAST MEETING, I WENT ONLINE, PROFESSOR.
AND YOU WERE RIGHT: FIFTEEN CRIMINAL SCIENTISTS HAVE VANISHED WITHOUT A TRACE SINCE THE BIG SUPERHERO CRISIS.
I THINK YOU'RE ON TO SOMETHING BUT I'M TRYING TO STAY AWAY FROM THAT WHOLE WORLD RIGHT NOW.
YOU DON'T KNOW WHAT IT'S LIKE OUT THERE SINCE LEX LUTHOR FIGURED OUT HOW TO GIVE SUPERPOWERS TO ANYONE WHO WANTS THEM.
NO ONE KNOWS WHAT'S GOING TO HAPPEN NEXT.
AND EVERY-BODY'S WATCHING EVERYBODY ELSE.
OUR AGENT HAS SUCCESSFULLY INSTALLED THE EQUIPMENT INTO PROFESSOR MORROW'S CELL AT HAVEN SECURITY VILLAGE, AS YOU CAN CLEARLY SEE, GREAT ONE.
IF IT'S ALL RIGHT TO CALL YOU "GREAT ONE."
I'M FINE WITH THAT.
NOW GO!
TELL THESE MONSTERS TO STUDY THEIR TARGETS WELL...

THEY'RE LOCKED IN, JOHN...
...AND THESE GUYS AREN'T GIVING UP.
BOOOMMM
WE COULD MOVE FASTER IF WE WEREN'T TRYING TO BRING *EVIL STAR'S* WHOLE SHIP IN.
YOU'VE GOT A POINT.
YOU THINKING WHAT I AM?
BABOOOMM
ON OCCASION.

GOT YA.
RING. INITIATE CODE TEN-TWELVE.
INCINERATE ALL EXTRATERRESTRIAL WEAPONS AND TECHNOLOGY.
INCINERATING.
JOHN, GET EVIL STAR OUT OF HERE.
I'LL HOLD THEM B--
--ACK--!

KRAKOOOOOOM
BLACK ADAM?
WE'VE GOT ENOUGH PROBLEMS HERE. WHAT DO YOU WANT?
SURELY YOU "POLICEMEN" ARE AWARE OF THE RECENT COALITION FORMED BETWEEN KAHNDAQ, NORTH KOREA AND MYANMAR.
THE CHINESE GOVERNMENT JOINED THAT COALITION TWO HOURS AGO.
YOU ATTACK THEM, YOU ATTACK ME.
ENTERING CHINA'S AIRSPACE IS NOW CONSIDERED A VIOLATION OF OUR FREEDOM OF POWER TREATY.
WE'RE NOT ATTACKING ANYONE, ADAM.
YOU WILL RETREAT IMMEDIATELY.
OR YOU CAN BOTH TRY WEARING THOSE RINGS WITHOUT HANDS.
WHOOOOM

<BY ORDER OF THE RUSSIAN GOVERNMENT, WE HAVE BEEN AUTHORIZED TO ALLOW THE GREEN LANTERNS SAFE PASSAGE INTO OUR COUNTRY'S AIRSPACE.>
<AUGUST GENERAL IN IRON TO GREAT WALL, WE...>
<POSITION TO CONTINUE PURSUIT INTO RUSSIAN AIRSPACE.>
<AWAITING BLACK ADAM'S ORDERS.>
<THE GREAT WALL DENIES THAT REQUEST, IMMORTAL-MAN-IN-DARKNESS.>
I'VE SEEN YOU MOUTHING OFF ON TELEVISION. TEARING A MAN IN HALF TO MAKE A POINT. THAT THE WORLD IS TOO SOFT ON "SUPER-VILLAINS."
A TAD THEATRICAL.
WHAT ARE YOU TRYING TO BUILD, ADAM?

THE COALITION HAS JUST BEGUN, GREEN LANTERNS.
ALREADY, I AM IN TALKS WITH THE GOVERNMENTS OF IRAN, PAKISTAN, UZBEKISTAN--
--AND RUSSIA. THE ROCKET REDS WILL JOIN US SOON ENOUGH.
YOUR DAYS OF AMERICA USING THIS WORLD AS YOUR PERSONAL BATTLEGROUND ARE OVER.
STAY IN YOUR OWN COUNTRY. LEAVE THE REST OF US ALONE.
YOU DO REALIZE WHAT YOU'RE DOING, ADAM.
YOU'RE TAKING IT UPON YOURSELF TO REPRESENT THIS COALITION.
THAT MEANS YOU FLY ONE FOOT IN HERE AND YOU'VE JUST COMMITTED AN ACT OF WAR.
AND WE DON'T WANT THAT...
...DO WE?

NO TRESPASSING
Week 6 Day 2
Arizona
WHAT'S HE PREPARING FOR? WORLD WAR III?
AN UNDERGROUND CONCRETE BUNKER IN THE MIDDLE OF THE DESERT? THIS WAS HIS LAST KNOWN ADDRESS?
WELL, TO HIS CREDIT, SIR, DOCTOR RIP HUNTER IS JUST BEING SAFE.
HE IS THE FATHER OF TIME TRAVEL. THUS, OVER SEVENTY-NINE ATTEMPTS HAVE BEEN MADE TO STEAL HIS TEMPORAL MACHINES DURING THE LAST YEAR ALONE.
NOT TO MENTION THE PRICES MANY ARE WILLING TO PAY FOR THE BLUEPRINTS TO HIS TIME SPHERE, THE TIME CAPSULE MINUTEMEN OR ANY OF HIS OTHER INVENTIONS.
HELLO!? RIP?!
IT'S BOOSTER GOLD!
PERHAPS HE ISN'T HOME.
THAT WOULD EXPLAIN WHY I COULDN'T REACH HIM EARLIER.
NOK
NOK
OR MAYBE HE'S CAUGHT UP IN ONE OF HIS PROJECTS.
SKEETS, WHAT KIND OF LOCK IS THAT?
AN ATOMIC TIME LOCK, SIR.
418009178
80977320
216811900
A TIME LOCK? WHEN'S IT SET TO OPEN?
MIDNIGHT, JANUARY, FIRST...
...FIFTY-TWO B.C.
I HATE TIME TRAVELERS.
DOCTOR RIP HUNTER SET THE LOCK, BUT ITS COMPUTER CHIPS WERE MANUFACTURED BY KORD OMNIVERSAL.
SO TECHNICALLY SPEAKING, THAT MEANS THE CENTRAL PROCESSOR IS MY GREAT, GREAT, GREAT, GREAT, GREAT GRANDFATHER.
IT SPEAKS A PRIMITIVE LANGUAGE, BUT I THINK I CAN CONVINCE IT TO OPEN UP IF I JUST...
KLANK
YOU'RE MAGIC, SKEETS.
THANK YOU, SIR.
UNFORTUNATELY, THE LOCK HAS A FAILSAFE REQUIRING A CONSTANT HARDWIRE SEQUENCING CODE TO KEEP IT OPEN.
I'M AFRAID I MUST REMAIN HERE.
NO PROBLEM. I'M SURE THERE'S NOTHING TO BE...

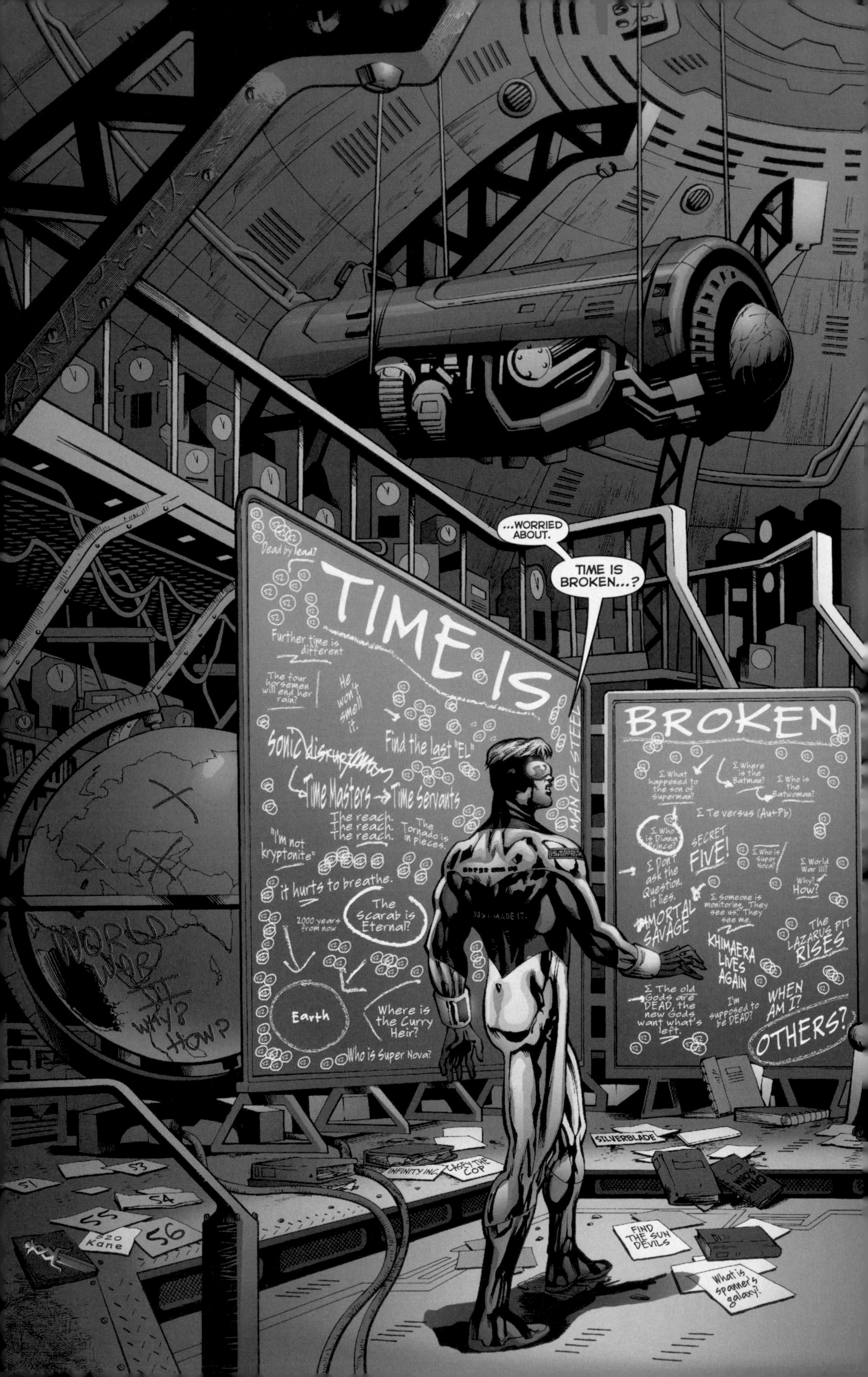

...WORRIED ABOUT.
TIME IS BROKEN...?
Dead by lead?
TIME IS
Further time is different
The four horsemen will end her rain?
He won't smell it.
Find the last "EL"
Time Masters → Time Servants
The reach. The reach. The reach.
The Tornado is in pieces.
"I'm not kryptonite"
it hurts to breathe.
The Scarab is Eternal?
2000 years from now
Earth
Where is the Curry Heir?
Who is Super Nova?
MAN OF STEEL
BROKEN
Σ What happened to the son of Superman?
Σ Where is the Batman?
Σ Who is the Batwoman?
Σ Te versus (Au+Pb)
Σ Who is Diana Prince?
SECRET FIVE!
Σ Who is Super Nova?
Σ World War III? Why? How?
Σ Don't ask the Question. It lies.
Σ Someone is monitoring. They see us. They see me.
IMMORTAL SAVAGE
KHIMAERA LIVES AGAIN
The LAZARUS PIT RISES
Σ The old Gods are DEAD, the new Gods want what's left.
I'm supposed to be DEAD?
WHEN AM I?
OTHERS?
WORLD WAR III why? HOW?
SILVERBLADE
INFINITY INC.
CASEY THE COP
51
53
54
55
56
520 Kane
FIND THE SUN DEVILS
What is spanner's galaxy?

SUN
7053

"IT'S ALL HIS FAULT"?
WHOSE FAULT? WHO--?
IS ALL HIS FAULT
HIS FAULT
IT'S HIS FAULT
HIS FAULT
...ME?!
UP IN THE SKY: CITY'S NEW HERO IS GOLD!
IT'S HIS FAULT!
NEXT IN

WEEK SIX NOTES

KEITH GIFFEN

I deliberately stayed away from the weekly conference calls, told myself that not knowing exactly what was coming on any given week would keep me fresh. I knew the overall but tried to steer clear of the details. That strategy really paid off in this issue. The Great Ten, Rip Hunter's enigmatic messages, Booster paying off a super villain shill...I felt like a fan again. I think this is the issue that got me really believing we were going to pull this off...kinda.

The weekly machine was chugging along pretty nicely by this issue. I'd pretty much settled into a visual rhythm, the Big Four were getting more comfortable with the weekly round robin structure (at least that's how it felt to me), and the artists were handing in some of the best work of their careers. That said, this was still only the sixth issue and, truth be told, I was still pretty concerned about down the line, when the "bloom's off the rose."

Small confession here. I was a bit disappointed when I first saw this issue's cover. Front loading Green Lantern seemed, to me, unnecessary. I thought the Great Ten should have been placed up front and center. Shows how much I know. Issue six's cover turned out to be an across the board favorite. Sorry, J.G., It won't happen again.

MARK WAID

The notes on the blackboard in Rip Hunter's lab came mostly out of Wacker's head, culled from his knowledge of where each plotline was going (at the time). I will tell you right now that, despite our best intentions, we never got around to addressing "2000 years from now" or "What is Spanner's Galaxy?", so stop holding your breath. Absolutely no one, no one, commented on the presence of Professor Hyatt's Time Pool magnet. Their oversight.

Socialist Red Guardsman

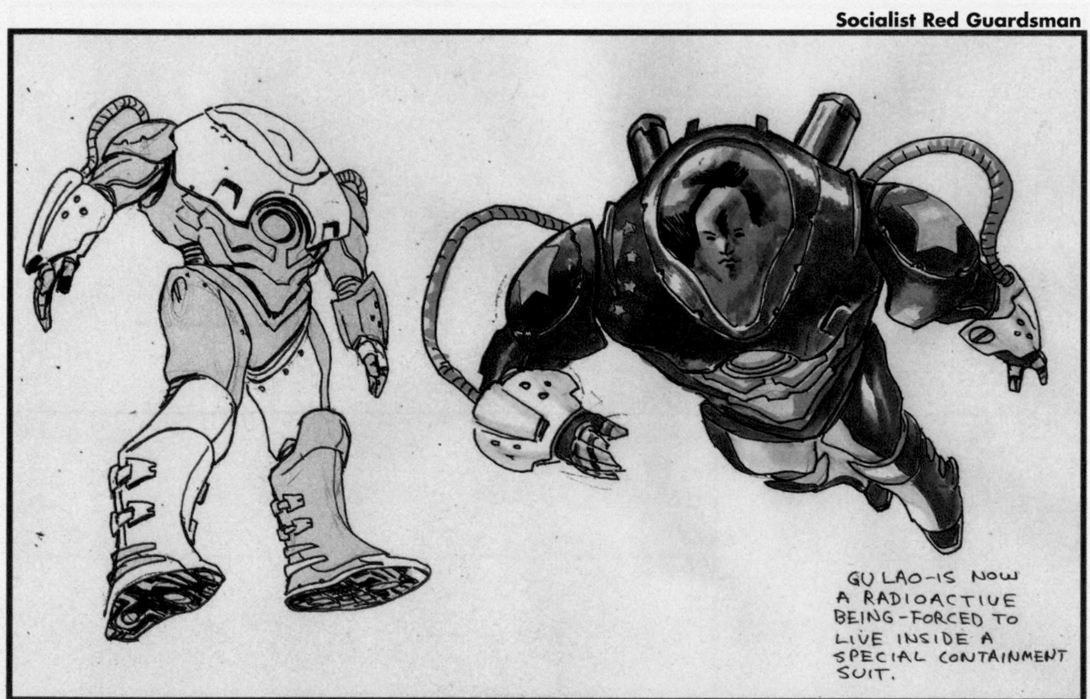

GU LAO-IS NOW
A RADIOACTIVE
BEING-FORCED TO
LIVE INSIDE A
SPECIAL CONTAINMENT
SUIT.

August General in Iron

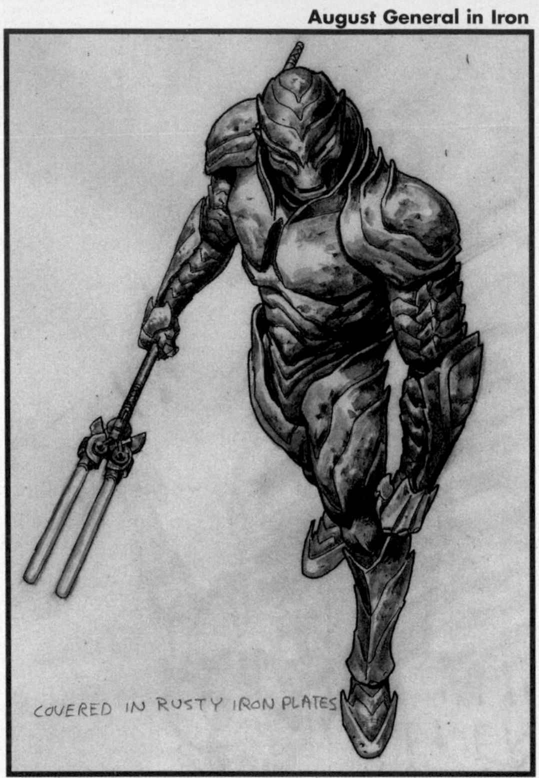

Celestial Archer

Accomplished Perfect Physician

one of the Seven Brothers

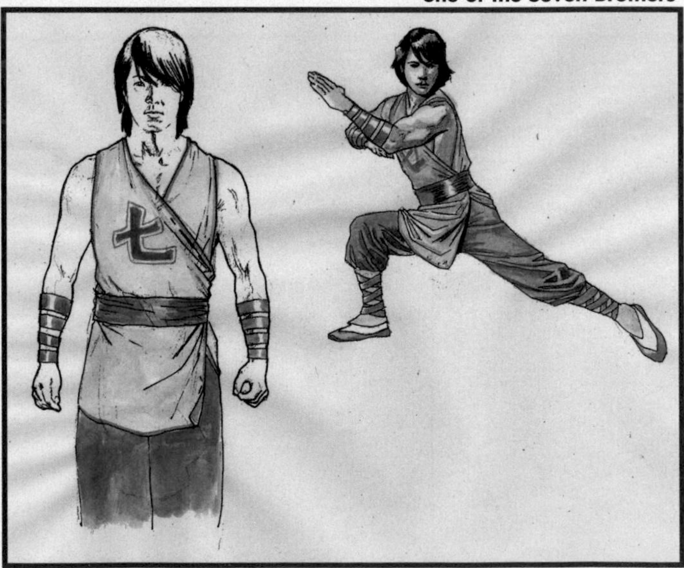

GREAT TEN

DESIGNS BY **J.G. JONES**

Immortal Man in Darkness

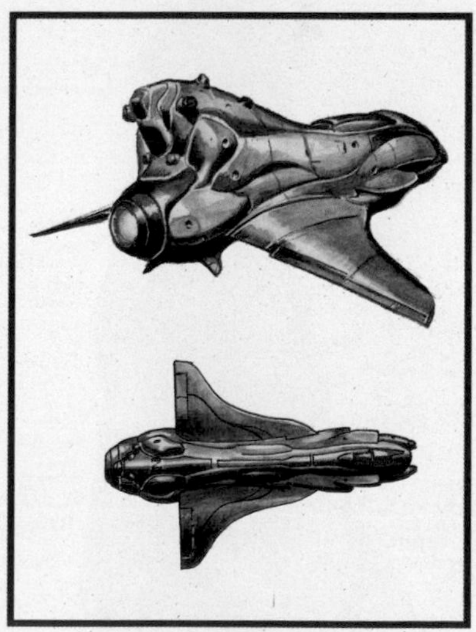

Thundermind

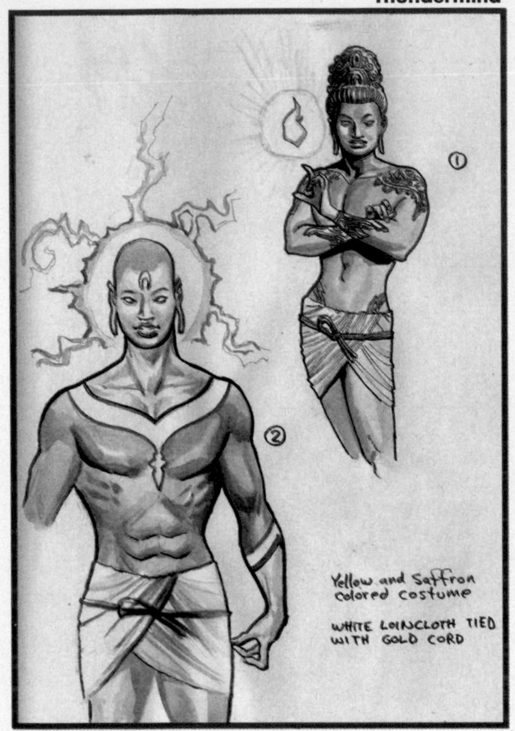

Ghost Fox Killer

Mother of Champions

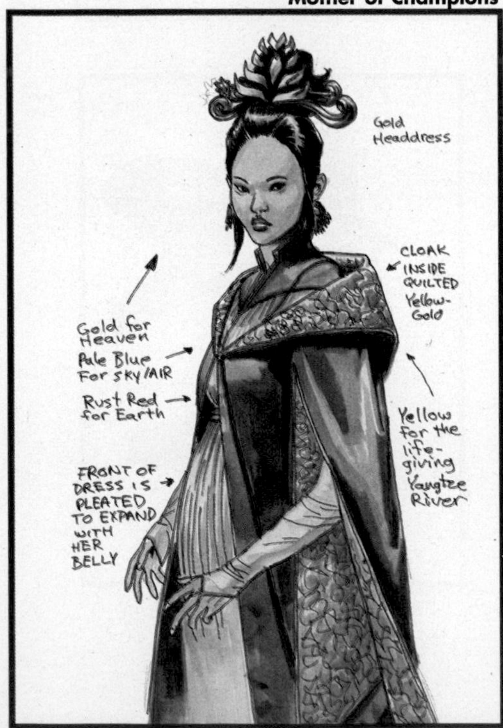

Shaolin Robot

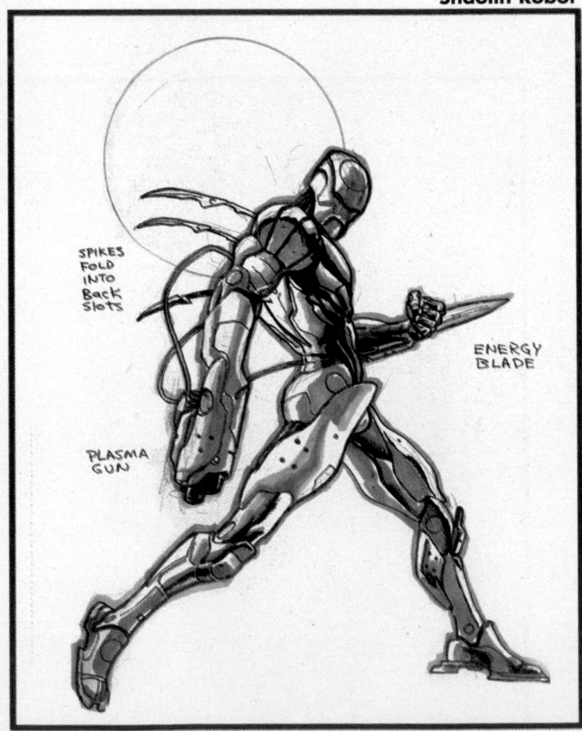

ANYONE?
Week 7 Week 7 Week 7 Week 7
GOING DOWN
I COULD USE SOME HELP HERE.
Writers: Johns, Morrison, Rucka, Waid
Layouts: Giffen
Art: Lashley & Draxhall
Colors: Sinclair
Letters: Lanham
Cover: Jones & Sinclair
Asst. Editors: Jones & Richards
Editor: Wacker
THERE'S SOMETHING HERE WITH US ON THIS PLANET, AND WE HAVE TO GET OFF BEFORE IT WAKES UP.
YOU HEARD WHAT BUDDY SAID, AND THE GUY'S GOT ANIMAL SENSES, RIGHT ?
DON'T BRING ME INTO IT.
YOU GUYS WANNA FIGHT, GO FOR IT.
I THINK WE MAY AS WELL JUST STAY HERE UNTIL WE'RE RESCUED.
THAT THING'S NOT SPACEWORTHY.
AND AFTER ALL WE'VE BEEN THROUGH, I NEED THIS VACATION.

WHAT IS IT YOU'RE TRYING TO DO HERE, ANYWAY?
CATAPULT US INTO SPACE WITH VINES?
YEAH, WELL, THAT'S PLAN B IF YOU PEOPLE DON'T GET UP OFF YOUR BACKSIDES!

YOU KNOW SOMETHING?
THIS FRUIT YOU'RE EATING!
IT'S CHANGING YOU!

WHAT DO YOU KNOW, ADAM STRANGE?
YOU DON'T KNOW HOW DELICIOUS IT IS BECAUSE YOU WON'T EAT ANY!

GOOD. USE THAT BRAIN OF YOURS AND THINK.
SURE, YOU CAN FLY IN SPACE, PRINCESS, BUT YOU CAN'T ACCELERATE TO ANYWHERE NEAR THE TRANSLIGHT SPEEDS IT'S GONNA TAKE TO GET US HOME TO OUR FAMILIES.
...YOU WON'T EAT ANY...

FACE IT, THIS BROKEN-DOWN, BEAT-UP THANAGARIAN WARBIRD IS OUR LAST CHANCE.
SO MAYBE YOU COULD HELP LOCATE THAT MYSTERIOUS POWER OUTPUT WE DETECTED.

...I...
I...THINK I NEED TO CLEAR MY HEAD...
BE MY GUEST, PRINCESS.
BUT GET BACK SOON--WE'RE LAUNCHING BEFORE SUNDOWN.

Week 7, Day 2
Father's Day was this past Sunday.
Gotham City.

I didn't bother to send a card.
I haven't spoken to my father in over eighteen months. Haven't spoke to my mother in twice that long.

What do they expect? They disowned me.
That's not the point.

The point is that Father's Day gets me thinking about family.
Folks who have them. Folks who don't.
I'm guessing the no-face guy doesn't have much family, either.

Then again, I kinda dig the idea of his no-face mama raising a brood of no-faced kids.

If I ever see his annoying lack-of-face again, maybe I'll ask him.
Then again, if I ever see him again, maybe I'll just belt him across his lack of a mouth.
Black Adam promise to change world
TERRA MAN DEAD!
CROWDS GATHER AT LUTHOR HQ
520 Kane St
?

That seems unlikely. It's been three weeks since I saw Mister cryptic-I-have-no-face-but-plenty-of-attitude.
Three weeks since I almost died in some hideout and I still don't even know why.

No answers.
Nothing but three cracked ribs, a fractured elbow, and a gun off the set of Rangers From Tomorrow to show for it.

I $@€#ing hate that show.

Time to walk away.
Captain Sawyer was right, I'm not a P.I., I don't owe this no-face guy anything.
Besides, he only paid for three weeks' work, and I've put in more like six, now.

Thing is, I know I'm missing something.
A clue or a lead or... something.

Something simple. Something obvious.
Something right under my...
GOTHAM GOSSIP
Past due

GOSSIP
due
FAMILY
GALA.
...nose....

...I am so stupid...
...Kate...

...it's been a long time, Kate....
GOTHAM GOSSIP
CATWOMAN "ROBS" PHARMACY
KANE FAMILY CHARITY GALA.

STOP CALLING.
I WANT MY MONEY, CHUMP.
TEN MINUTES, SIR.
ON IT, YOU VULTURE.
YOU'D BETTER BE.
LAST WARNING, GOLD. AND DON'T CALL ME A VULTURE.
KNOCK
KNOCK KNOCK

NINE MINUTES.
NOT YOU. SKEETS.
SKEETS, GET THE DOOR!
NO HANDS, SIR!
KNOCK KNOCK KNOCK
AND YOU-- YOU HANG ON--!
NO.
Klik

RALPH?
BOOSTER. BAD TIME?

YOU WOULDN'T BELIEVE THE IRONY OF THAT QUESTION IF I TOLD YOU.
HELLO? HELLO?
HEY, SKEETS, GET THE WORLD-FAMOUS ELONGATED MAN HERE SOMETHING TO DRINK!
AGAIN, SIR, NO HANDS.
EIGHT MINUTES.

THIS ISN'T A SOCIAL CALL, BOOSTER. I'M INVESTIGATING A RESURRECTIONIST SECT CALLED THE CULT OF CONNER.
I'VE TRAILED THEM HERE TO METROPOLIS, AND --
BEEP BEEP
UH-HUH. HELP YOURSELF TO THE FRIDGE, RALPH. I'LL BE RIGHT WITH YOU.
C'MON, YOU EXTORTIONIST, PICK UPPPP...

BOOSTER, PAY ATTENTION. THIS IS IMPORTANT.
THE NUMBER YOU HAVE DIALED IS NOT IN SERVICE.
WHAT? BUT HE JUST CALLED--?
BOOSTER!

RALPH, I HAVE MY OWN CASES RIGHT NOW, BUT IF I HEAR ANYTHING ABOUT THIS CONDOR CULT, I'LL--
CONNER. AS IN CONNER A.K.A. THE LATE SUPERBOY.
THESE "CASES"--ARE YOU DEFENDING PEOPLE IN NEED OR GREEDY MARKETERS?

I'M INSULTED. WITH SUPERMAN GONE, RALPH, SOMEONE'S GOT TO STEP UP TO THE PLATE IN METROPOLIS, AND I DON'T SEE YOU DOING IT.
GO ONLINE AND CHECK OUT THE DAILY PLANET SOMETIME. I STOPPED A PSYCHO NAMED MANTHRAX JUST LAST WEEK. IT WAS A HUGE DEAL.
LOOK, I'M STACKED UP. IF YOU STILL NEED HELP, CALL ME NEXT WEEK--WAIT--THE WEEK AFTER.
THREE MINUTES, SIR.

THREE MINUTES TO WHAT, SKEETS?
TELL HIM. HE CAN KEEP A SECRET.
WHERE ARE MY GOGGLES...?
AROUND YOUR NECK, SIR.

ACCORDING TO THE HISTORICAL RECORDS IN MY DATABANKS, MR. DIBNY, TONIGHT'S HEADLINES TELL OF A MASSIVE OUTBREAK OF MOB VIOLENCE OUTSIDE THE LEXCORP BUILDING.
WITH ADVANCE WARNING, BOOSTER CAN BE ON THE SCENE BEFORE TRUE CARNAGE ERUPTS.

THAT'S RIGHT. SKEETS, YOU'VE BEEN GONE SO LONG, I THINK WE ALL FORGOT...YOU AND BOOSTER ARE FROM THE 25TH CENTURY.
THAT'S HOW BOOSTER'S ALWAYS THERE TO PREVENT THE BIG CRIMES AND DISASTERS IN METROPOLIS. HE KNOWS ABOUT THEM IN ADVANCE.

THIS WHOLE ERA IS HISTORY TO YOU. DATA.
SO IF THAT'S THE CASE...

WHAM
...WHY THE HELL DIDN'T YOU WARN ME MY WIFE WAS GOING TO DIE?

RA-- KOFF RALPH, I WAS AS SURPRISED AS YOU! I SWEAR!
I DIDN'T LEARN EVERY LITTLE DETAIL--

LITTLE DETAIL?
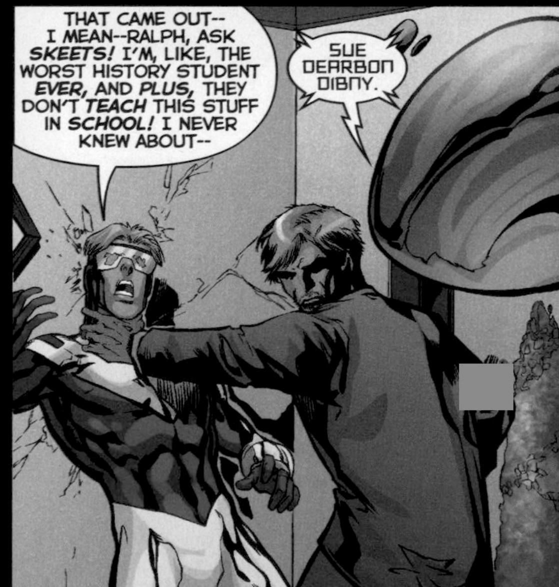
THAT CAME OUT-- I MEAN--RALPH, ASK SKEETS! I'M, LIKE, THE WORST HISTORY STUDENT EVER, AND PLUS, THEY DON'T TEACH THIS STUFF IN SCHOOL! I NEVER KNEW ABOUT--
SUE DEARBON DIBNY.

MURDERED EIGHT MONTHS AGO BY JEAN LORING. A PIVOTAL EVENT IN THE 21ST CENTURY SUPER-HERO COMMUNITY.
TWO MINUTES, SIR.

RALPH, I WASN'T KEEPING THAT FROM YOU. IT'S JUST...WHY WOULD I EVEN THINK TO ASK...?
NO, IT'S MY FAULT.
Whew.
FOR THINKING YOU WOULD THINK.

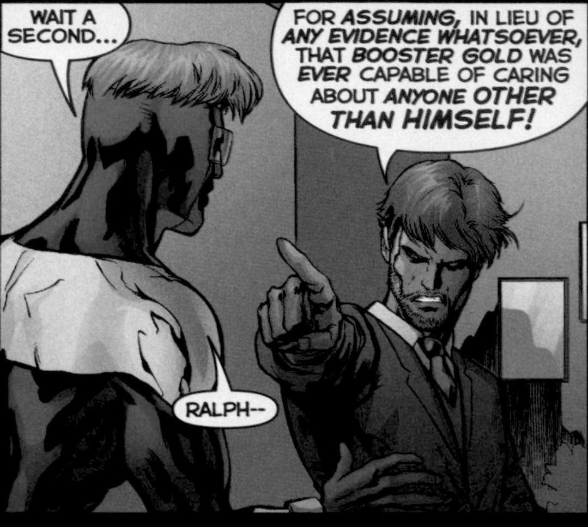
WAIT A SECOND...
FOR ASSUMING, IN LIEU OF ANY EVIDENCE WHATSOEVER, THAT BOOSTER GOLD WAS EVER CAPABLE OF CARING ABOUT ANYONE OTHER THAN HIMSELF!
RALPH--

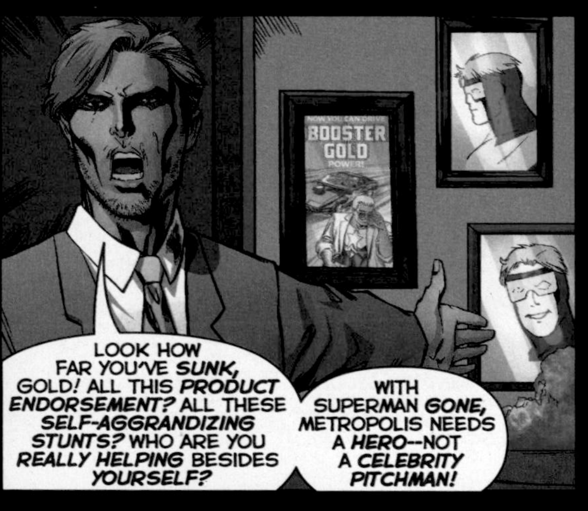
BOOSTER GOLD
LOOK HOW FAR YOU'VE SUNK, GOLD! ALL THIS PRODUCT ENDORSEMENT? ALL THESE SELF-AGGRANDIZING STUNTS? WHO ARE YOU REALLY HELPING BESIDES YOURSELF?
WITH SUPERMAN GONE, METROPOLIS NEEDS A HERO--NOT A CELEBRITY PITCHMAN!

I DO THE JOB, WHICH IS MORE THAN I CAN SAY FOR A "JUSTICE LEAGUER" WHO HASN'T SUITED UP IN EIGHT MONTHS!
DON'T THINK BECAUSE I PITY YOU, I'M GONNA TAKE ANY CRAP OFF YOU! YOU'RE LOOKING AT SUPERMAN'S REPLACEMENT RIGHT HERE, RALPH!

BOOM

PROVE IT.

I showered twice, I did my hair, I ironed my shirt, I shined my boots.
Hell, I even used my fancy soap.

I'm telling myself that I did these things because I'm being respectful of the wealth and power I'm about to drop in on unannounced.
Kane Estate
I did these things because of that, and not because I'm going to see her.

Yeah. I don't buy it, either.
The square badges on the gate know I don't belong.
I'M SORRY, THIS IS BY INVITATION ONLY.
As always, they delight in pointing out that kind of thing.

It's been the better part of ten years.
YEAH, IT ALWAYS IS.

LISTEN, JUST CALL UP TO THE HOUSE AND LET KATHERINE THE YOUNGER KNOW THAT OFFICER RENEE IS HERE.
THAT WOULD BE YOU?
JUST GIVE HER THE MESSAGE.

It takes three minutes for permission to approach the house, another five just to walk up the damn driveway.
THIS WAY, PLEASE.
I try to calculate exactly how much money I pass on my way in, and give up at fifty million.

The name is Kane, but the money is Hamilton.
The Hamilton Rifle Company, to be exact.

Like trying to calculate the money, you can't begin to count the dead.
IF YOU'LL WAIT HERE, PLEASE...

After a certain number, both lose all meaning.
...MISTRESS KANE WILL BE WITH YOU IN A MOMENT.
THANKS, JEEVES.

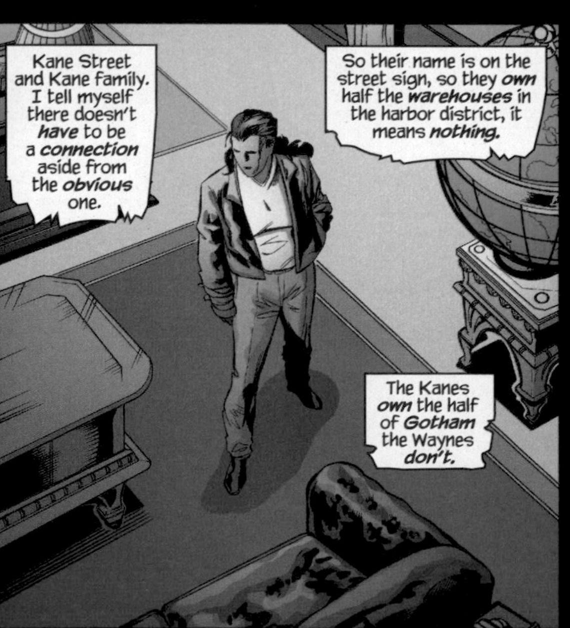
Kane Street and Kane family. I tell myself there doesn't have to be a connection aside from the obvious one.
So their name is on the street sign, so they own half the warehouses in the harbor district, it means nothing.
The Kanes own the half of Gotham the Waynes don't.

I've convinced myself that sneaking out the servants' entrance is a good idea when I hear her voice...
IF YOU'VE COME TO ARREST ME, OFFICER MONTOYA...

...by which time it's *far* too late for me to do *anything* except *stare.*

...I TRUST YOU'LL BE *SEARCHING* ME *FIRST?*

IF YOU *INSIST...*

Pictures *never* do her *justice.*

Kate Kane has the kind of beauty that leaves you *breathless...*
...THOUGH THAT *DRESS* ISN'T LIKELY TO *CONCEAL* ANYTHING I HAVEN'T *SEEN* BEFORE.
GUARDIAN CIGARETTES

...and the kind of *temper* that leaves you *bruised.*

It's a *good* hit. I feel the *blood* filling my *mouth.*
YOU'VE GOT A *LOT* OF *NERVE,* COMING *HERE.*
ESPECIALLY AFTER THE *LAST* TIME I SAW *YOU.*
Somewhere along the line, someone *taught* her how to *throw* a *punch.*

Fortunately, I learned a long time ago how to take one.
I ASSUME THIS MEANS YOU'RE STILL IN THE CLOSET?

It's an easy button to press.
YOU SELF-RIGHTEOUS--
This time, I see the response coming.

I could always press her buttons.
NOT SO LOUD...

And she could always press mine.
...SOMEONE MIGHT COME IN HERE AND GET THE WRONG IDEA.

That's what made it so good.

That's why it couldn't last.
WHAT DO YOU WANT, RENEE?
YOU'RE NOT ON THE FORCE ANYMORE, WHY ARE YOU HERE?
At least, that's what we told ourselves.

BEEN ASKING ABOUT ME, HAVE YOU?
DON'T FLATTER YOURSELF.
FATHER HAD COMMISSIONER AKINS AND HIS WIFE TO DINNER LAST MONTH, IT CAME UP IN CONVERSATION.

I'M ASKING AGAIN, WHY ARE YOU HERE?
FIVE-TWENTY KANE STREET. IT'S IN THE HARBOR DISTRICT.
DO I LOOK LIKE I SPEND MY TIME IN THE HARBOR DISTRICT?

YOU LOOK LIKE YOU SPEND YOUR TIME AT CALAIS ON 63RD, GETTING MUD BATHS, MASSAGES, AND FACIALS.
BUT THE BUILDING, FIVE-TWENTY, YOUR FAMILY STILL OWNS IT?

I DON'T KNOW. POSSIBLY. PROBABLY.

COULD YOU FIND OUT?
DOES THIS HAVE ANYTHING TO DO WITH THAT CAST YOU'RE SPORTING?
I NEED TO KNOW, KATE. CALL IT CURIOSITY.
WHY SHOULD I HELP YOU?

BECAUSE ONCE WE THOUGHT WE WERE IN LOVE WITH EACH OTHER.
AND MAYBE WE EVEN WERE.

It's the wrong thing to say.
Unfortunately, I realize that after I've said it.

I THINK YOU HAD BETTER GO NOW.
KATE...
GO...

...BEFORE I CHANGE MY MIND AND DECIDE NOT TO HELP YOU.

YOU CAN SHOW YOURSELF OUT.
YOU KNOW WHERE TO FIND ME?
YES...

...I ALWAYS HAVE...

Metropolis.

TRUCK JUST *JACKKNIFED*

OUTTA *MY WAY*

I HEARD IT'S A *TEST*

BET WE'RE BEIN' WATCHED RIGHT *NOW*

WHO *CARES? MOVE,* JACKASS!

ONE SIDE, CITIZENS-- BUT READY YOUR *CAMERAS*--

--FOR *ONCE AGAIN,* IT'S *BOOSTER GOLD* TO THE *RESCUE!*

WHOOM

HE DIN'T *STOPPIT--!*
PLEASE, HOLD YOUR *APPLAUSE* UNTIL THE *BIG FINISH!* IN TWO... *ONE...*

...SUCCESS!
AND LET THIS BE A *REMINDER,* LADIES AND GENTLEMEN-- NEVER LEAVE YOUR HOUSE WITHOUT AN OFFICIAL *BOOSTER GOLD WINDPROOF UMBRELLA!*

BRAVO, SIR! WASN'T IT A THRILLING SIGHT, MR. DIBNY?
HARD TO TELL, SKEETS. I DIDN'T READY MY CAMERA.
BOOSTER! OVER HERE!
BEFORE WE START, MS...LANE, IS IT?... BRIEF ME.
AS I CAME IN, I OVERHEARD PEOPLE UNSURE THAT THEY WERE REALLY IN DANGER. WERE THEY THAT CONFUSED BY A BURNING TANKER?
THEY WERE WORRIED THAT IT WAS A PRE-SCREENING OF SOME SORT. WE'RE OUTSIDE THE LEXCORP BUILDING--AND THAT'S THE REASON THIS BLOCK IS SO CROWDED THIS TIME OF NIGHT.
APPARENTLY, LEX LUTHOR ANNOUNCED AN OPEN CALL FOR VOLUNTEERS TO PARTICIPATE IN HIS "SUPERGENE" TESTING PROGRAM.
I'VE SEEN THE ADS. THE WHOLE IDEA THAT LUTHOR'S GEARING UP TO, WHAT, "SELL" SUPER-POWERS IS CHILLING...
SIR, TWO OF OUR SPONSORS ARE LEXCORP AFFILIATES.
...BUT DON'T QUOTE ME.
I'M JUST GLAD I WAS ABLE TO FIND A WATER MAIN IN TIME TO SAVE ALL LIVES. STOPPING AN EXPLODING PROPANE TRUCK IS--
--AN AMAZING STUNT-- BUT I HAVE A QUESTION!
HOW MUCH DID IT COST YOU?

I HAVE...NO IDEA WHAT... YOU'RE TALKING ABOUT...
INTERVIEW'S OVER, FOLKS!
WE'LL DECIDE THAT, THANKS.
SIR, CAN I HAVE YOUR NAME?

IT'S BILL CASTELL, AND I'M AN ACTOR! LAST WEEK, BOOSTER GOLD HIRED ME TO STAGE A FAKE--
MS. LANE, DON'T LISTEN TO A WORD THAT MAN SAYS!

HE'S A PROVEN THREAT TO--
GO ON, MR. CASTELL!
--A FAKE ATTACK ON A COMMUTER RAIL--

--AND THEN HIS CHECK BOUNCED OVER THE BANK BUILDING IN A SINGLE BOUND!
I WARNED HIM! I SAID I KNEW I COULD GO TO JAIL FOR MY PART IN THIS--
--BUT I'LL DO IT TO DRAG THAT SON OF A BITCH DOWN!

ENOUGH, MR. CASTELL!
BOOSTER, IS THIS TRUE? DO YOU KNOW THIS MAN? WAS LAST WEEK'S SUBWAY RESCUE SIMPLY A PUBLICITY STUNT?

NO! I MEAN--THIS ISN'T LIKE IT SEEMS--
BOOSTER! GARY McCRAW, WGBS-TV! HOW MUCH DID YOU PAY CASTELL?
AMI SOON, CHANNEL FIVE! CAN YOU DISCREDIT THIS CLAIM?

RALPH DIBNY, HUMAN RACE.
HOW MANY OTHER OF THESE LAST SIX WEEKS' "DEATH-DEFYING RESCUES" HAVE YOU STAGED TO IMPROVE YOUR MARKETABILITY?

MR. DIBNY, AS ELONGATED MAN, YOU SERVED WITH BOOSTER GOLD IN THE JUSTICE LEAGUE. ARE YOU ALLEGING THAT HE'S CAPABLE OF FRAUD?
AS FAR AS I'M CONCERNED, ABSOLUTELY.
RALPH, SHUT THE HELL UP! I SWEAR, THIS ISN'T WHAT IT LOOKS LIKE!

TOO LITTLE, TOO LATE, GOLD. ALL CAMERAS, ALL MICROPHONES, RIGHT HERE, ON ME!
YOU CANNOT DEPEND ON THIS MAN! WHATEVER GOLD DOES, HE DOESN'T DO IT FOR YOU!
RALPH--
HE IS A VAIN OPPORTUNIST WHO POSES AS A HERO TO EARN LUCRATIVE CORPORATE CONTRACTS!

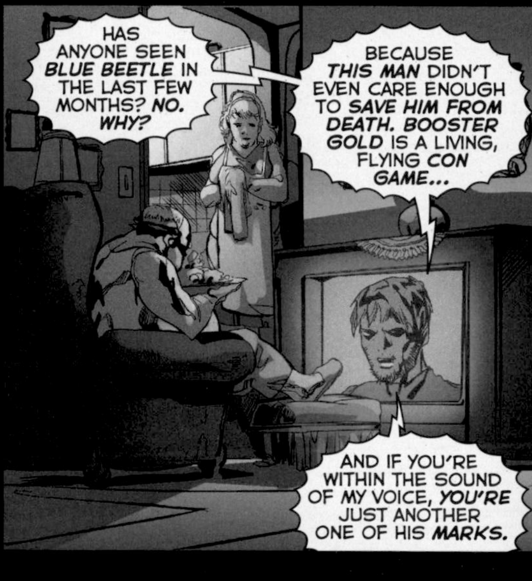
HAS ANYONE SEEN BLUE BEETLE IN THE LAST FEW MONTHS? NO. WHY?
BECAUSE THIS MAN DIDN'T EVEN CARE ENOUGH TO SAVE HIM FROM DEATH. BOOSTER GOLD IS A LIVING, FLYING CON GAME...
AND IF YOU'RE WITHIN THE SOUND OF MY VOICE, YOU'RE JUST ANOTHER ONE OF HIS MARKS.

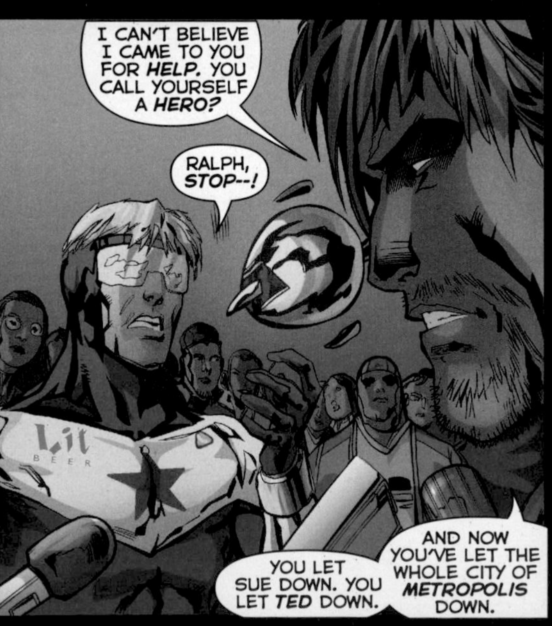
I CAN'T BELIEVE I CAME TO YOU FOR HELP. YOU CALL YOURSELF A HERO?
RALPH, STOP--!
Lit
BEER
YOU LET SUE DOWN. YOU LET TED DOWN.
AND NOW YOU'VE LET THE WHOLE CITY OF METROPOLIS DOWN.

YOU'RE PATHETIC.
MR. DIBNY, HOW LONG HAVE YOU BEEN AWARE OF GOLD'S THEATRICS?
WOULD YOU BE WILLING TO TESTIFY IN A CIVIL TRIAL AGAINST BOOSTER?
SIR?

NEXT IN

WEEK SEVEN NOTES

MARK WAID

For the first time, two of our plotlines intersect as Ralph comes calling on Booster Gold. As outlined in that week's conference call, their scenes were very tame and very polite. Consequently, once I rolled up my sleeves and began committing those scenes to paper, they were duller than dull. As Grant is fond of saying, super-hero comics are about characters in motion, and there is nothing intrinsically visual about two grown men having a well-mannered conversation while standing around a largely featureless apartment, floating robot-pal or no. Luckily, spurred on by my co-writers, I remembered two important lessons I'd learned about craft and applied them here with gusto.

Lesson One: Don't Be Afraid of Bruising the Apples. Because I've loved most of these characters since I was old enough to read, I sometimes have a tendency to treat them a little too gingerly, too familiarly. I had to keep reminding myself that Ralph was, at least for the time being, not the fun-loving, super-analytic detective I'd grown up with. He was an emotional wreck on the verge of having a total breakdown (see also Lesson Three: "Write What You Know"), and it was okay — in fact, more than okay — to have him explode with shocking outbursts and get physical so long as he remained fundamentally in character. Which leads us to:

Lesson Two: Walk Right Up to the Problem. As we broke this plot, Greg asked why, if Skeets and Booster both knew the future, they'd never warned Ralph of Sue's murder? (Greg always kept us grounded with anchors like "facts" and "realism," for which we were all honestly grateful.) We subsequently wasted a stupefying amount of time trying to invent cleverly unbreakable answers to this question, most all of them revolving around the unsatisfactory phrase, "Remember, Booster was a D-plus history student." Eventually, in desperation, just to see what energy it might stir, I elected to "hang a lantern" on the problem (a screenwriters' term for having the characters themselves ask the questions that are puzzling the audience), and suddenly the Booster/Ralph scenes had a whole new life to them. Some of my favorite bits I've ever written came about by availing myself of this gambit, so you'd think I wouldn't have to rediscover it every time I sit down to script. In return, I would remind you that being able to name twelve kinds of Kryptonite does not automatically make you a smart man.

One additional spoiler-alert note for those of you reading 52 for the first time: of course Booster's not stupid enough to pay a super-villain by check. Have faith, and keep reading.

B R E A K D O W N S

BY **KEITH GIFFEN**

Katherine "Kate" Kane makes her dramatic debut. The original script had her wearing a slinky, short party dress — which was later changed to the long, flowing red dress seen on page 155.

DC COMICS 52

Metropolis.
Steelworks.
NAT!
Week 8, Night 1

NATASHA!
IT'S TWO IN THE MORNING. DON'T YOU THINK IT'S TIME YOU GAVE YOURSELF A REST?
YOU GONNA MAKE ME A NEW SUIT OF ARMOR?
TIMES

NO.
CAN I GET THE METAGENE THERAPY, GET SOME REAL POWERS?
HELL NO.
THEN I'M NOT DONE, UNCLE JOHN.

FINE, I'M GOING TO BED.
TRY NOT TO BURN THE PLACE DOWN.

SHKZZZT

...FOR THE MORNING EDITION, BEGINNING AT SIX O'CLOCK.
WE'LL HAVE REPORTS ON THE LATEST DEVELOPMENTS IN THE BOOSTER GOLD FRAUD ALLEGATIONS, THE SLOWING RECOVERY EFFORT IN STAR CITY...
WHAT ALLEGATIONS? HE'S GUILTY AS SIN...
...AS WELL AS A LIVE INTERVIEW WITH LEX LUTHOR AND MORE ABOUT HIS "METAGENE FOR EVERYMAN" PROGRAM.
FROM ALL OF US AT W.L.I.I., GOODNIGHT, METROPOL--
KLIK
nnh
...NOT Hnnh AGAIN...
...WHAT THE HELL...?
TNK

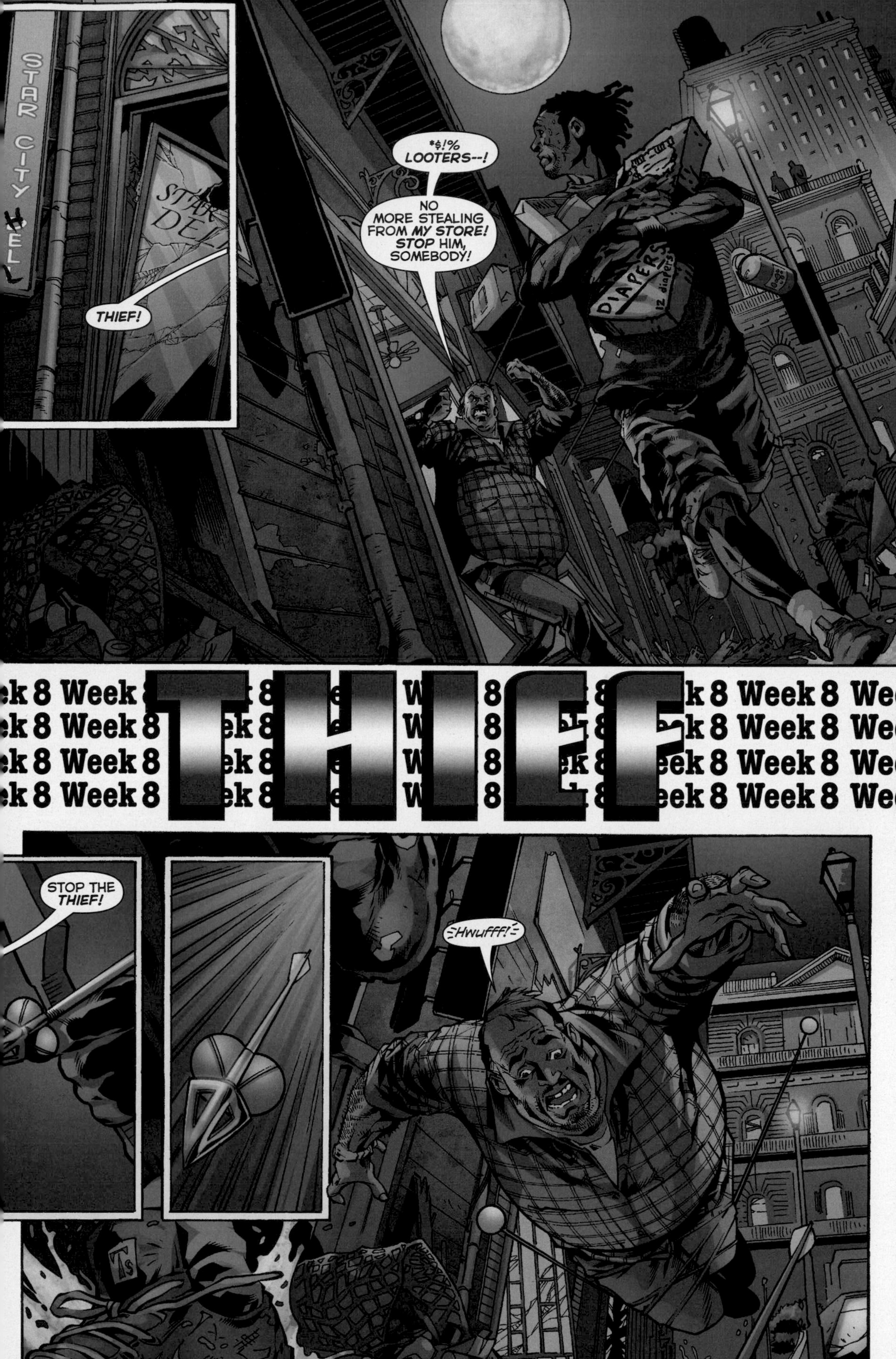
STAR CITY DELI
THIEF!
*$!% LOOTERS--!
NO MORE STEALING FROM MY STORE! STOP HIM, SOMEBODY!
DIAPERS 12 diapers
Week 8
THIEF
STOP THE THIEF!
Hwufff!

WRITTEN BY GEOFF JOHNS, GRANT MORRISON, GREG RUCKA, MARK WAID
ART BREAKDOWNS BY KEITH GIFFEN • PENCILS BY EDDY BARROWS
INKS BY ROB STULL • COLORS BY ALEX SINCLAIR

WE GOT THE *WORST* OF IT, THAT'S FOR DAMN SURE.
ENTIRE NEIGHBORHOODS LEVELED, SCHOOL SYSTEM BANKRUPT, PRIVATIZED POLICE BULLYING GOOD, FRIGHTENED FOLKS...

...AND, HIDDEN IN THE *SHADOWS* BECAUSE HE CAN'T FACE THE PEOPLE HE LET *DOWN*, A STUBBORN IDIOT WITH A *QUIVER* ON HIS BACK.
I WANT TO GET THIS CITY UP ON ITS *FEET* AGAIN, RALPH, BUT I *ASK* YOU:

LETTERING BY TRAVIS LANHAM • COVER BY J.G. JONES & ALEX SINCLAIR
ASSISTANT EDITORS JANN JONES & HARVEY RICHARDS
EDITED BY STEPHEN WACKER

WHAT CAN ONE MAN *DO?*

YOU KNOW THE ANSWER TO THAT, OLLIE. IN FACT, I SEEM TO REMEMBER YOU ASKING THAT EXACT SAME QUESTION ONCE *BEFORE.*

OH, *HO.* NOT FOR A *VERY* LONG...
RALPH, IF YOU'RE GETTING AT WHAT I *THINK* YOU'RE GETTING AT, THAT'S *CRAZY* TALK. WHAT ON *EARTH* MAKES YOU THINK I'D CONSIDER--
JUST A *SUGGESTION.* DON'T WANT IT, IGNORE IT. LET'S ATTACK *MY* PROBLEM. I'M HERE *LOOKING* FOR SOMEONE.
SOME *ONES.*

HOLY CRAP.
YEAH, ACTUALLY, THAT'S ESSENTIALLY MY READ ON IT, TOO.
MY WIFE'S TOMBSTONE WAS DEFACED BY AN UNDER-GROUND LUNATIC FRINGE CALLING ITSELF THE CULT OF CONNER.
I'D HEARD THEY'D SET UP A CHURCH HERE, AND APPARENTLY THAT WAS A SOLID LEAD.
THAT'S THEIR SIGN.
KRSH
EMPTY. SHOULD WE EXPECT THEM BACK?
NO. THEY TRAVEL. LIKE COCKROACHES. SCURRYING AT THE SLIGHTEST HINT OF EXPOSURE.
WHAT DO THEY WORSHIP, OR DO I WANNA KNOW?
RESURRECTION.
THEY BELIEVE THAT THE DECEASED CAN...
...
...CAN COME BACK FROM THE DEAD...

Week 8, Day 3
WHEN DID IT START, JOHN.
COUPLE DAYS AGO...
...IT'S BEEN PROGRESSING STEADILY SINCE SUNDAY.
IRONS, J.H. #002-A
BUT YOU HAVE BEEN ABLE TO CONTROL WHEN YOU... TRANSFORM?
AFTER INITIAL MANIFESTATION, TO AN EXTENT...
...I'M A LITTLE AFRAID OF WHAT WILL HAPPEN IF I TRY TO SWITCH FROM SOLID TO MOLTEN.
WHAT I DON'T HAVE IS ANY CONTROL OVER WHEN IT INITIALLY MANIFESTS.
IT SOUNDS ALIEN IN ORIGIN. HAVE YOU BEEN OFF-PLANET RECENTLY?
NEAR-ORBIT ONLY. I WAS PART OF THE STRIKE TEAM THAT KILLED BROTHER EYE...
ST★R

...I SUPPOSE IT COULD BE SOME MUTATION ON THE O.M.A.C.* VIRUS, THERE WAS THIS WOMAN WITH US--
NO, IT'S NOT O.M.A.C.-DERIVED. THERE'S A TOTAL ABSENCE OF ANY NANOBOT PRESENCE IN THE SAMPLE...
...INTERESTING...
*ONE MAN ARMY CORPS

...INCREDIBLY HIGH CONCENTRATIONS OF CHROMIUM, NICKEL, CARBON, AND IRON...
...WHAT DOES THAT MAKE...?
S.T.A.R.

STAINLESS STEEL.
I'M TURNING INTO STAINLESS STEEL.
JOHN, PLEASE, DON'T WORRY
THERE'S A CURE, THERE MUST BE, WE'LL FIND IT.
OH, I KNOW WHERE TO FIND IT.
I EVEN KNOW WHO DID IT TO ME, KALA.
STAINLESS STEEL...
...THAT'S LEX LUTHOR'S IDEA OF A JOKE.
HE MUST'VE DONE IT TO ME HERE, WHEN HE VISITED S.T.A.R. LABS WITH ALL THOSE REPORTERS.
"HE PUT HIS ARM AROUND ME...
"...THAT'S WHEN HE MUST'VE DONE IT...
"...INJECTED ME WITH SOMETHING, MOST LIKELY..."
...SOMETHING THAT EITHER TRIGGERED MY METAGENE...OR INFECTED ME WITH ONE...

...WHICH MEANS HE CAN TAILOR THE RESULTS.
BUT WHY?
VMMM

WHY WOULD HE DO THIS TO YOU WHEN HE HAS THOUSANDS OF PEOPLE LINING UP TO BECOME THE NEXT SUPERMAN?
WHY YOU?
TO PUNISH ME.
WHAT DO YOU THINK HIS METAGENE PROGRAM IS, KALA? LEX DOESN'T WANT TO CREATE SUPERMEN...

...HE WANTS TO CONTROL THEM.
WHY IS THE ALARM...?

LOOK OUT!

JOHN!!

THE SAMPLES!!

"...HAPPENED JUST LIKE I SAID. IF PEOPLE WAS YELLIN'... I DIN' HEAR NOTHIN' 'COUNTA MY GRANDSON THROWIN' A FIT 'BOUT SOMETHIN' OR 'NOTHER, YOU KNOW KIDS.
"ANYWAYS, ONE SECOND WE WAS THERE ON THE SIDEWALK...
"...WHEN I FEEL THIS HAND GRABBIN' MY SHOULDER, RIGHT?...

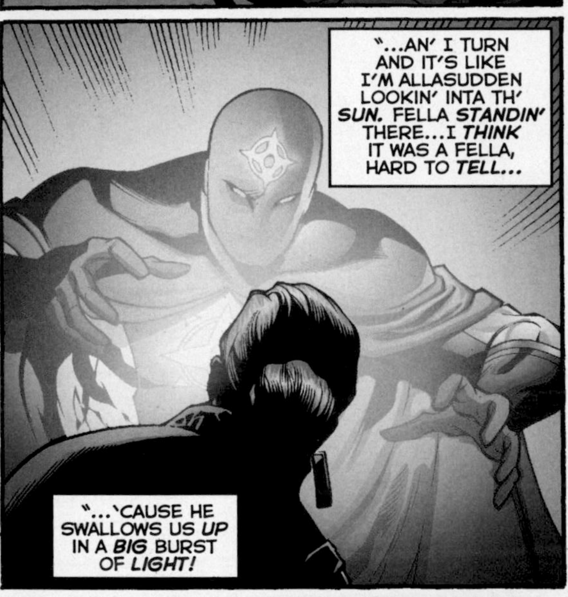
"...AN' I TURN AND IT'S LIKE I'M ALLASUDDEN LOOKIN' INTA TH' SUN. FELLA STANDIN' THERE...I THINK IT WAS A FELLA, HARD TO TELL...
"...'CAUSE HE SWALLOWS US UP IN A BIG BURST OF LIGHT!

"DOESN'T BURN OR NOTHIN'... BUT HALF A SECOND LATER, WHEN MY EYES IS CLEAR, WE'S ALTOGETHER ACROSS THE STREET...AN' WHERE WE BEEN STANDIN'..."

...WELL... SEE FOR YOURSELF.
WHOEVER HE WAS, HE SAVED OUR 'LIVES.
BUT I'LL BE HONEST, MISTER...

Week 8, Day 4

Week 8, Day 5

...AND IF I HAVE TO HEAR *ONE MORE WORD* ABOUT THIS GUY, I'M GOING TO PUNCH YOU IN THE *NECK.*

SIR, *PLEASE*...YOUR *IMAGE*...
...IS IN THE *TOILET,* SKEETS, SO WHAT DAMAGE IS LEFT TO BE *DONE?*
ONE WEEK, BOOSTER GOLD IS METROPOLIS'S FAVORITE *HERO*...THE *NEXT,* SOME *NEW* BOY SCOUT HAS MOVED IN WHILE *I'M* GIVEN THE *HEAVE-HO!*

SIR, THIS MAN'S TAKING *NOTES*...!
"THIS MAN" IS GOING TO WRITE WHATEVER HE *FEELS* LIKE SO LONG AS IT SELLS *PAPERS.* HE DIDN'T COME TO *QUIZ ME* ON *CAPTAIN NEWGUY.*
GOLD
TARNISHED
HE CAME TO RUB MY *FACE* IN THIS WEEK'S *HEADLINES.* ISN'T THAT *RIGHT,* PAL?
OR HAVE YOU ACTUALLY GATHERED SOME *FACTS* FOR A CHANGE? HUH? WHAT ABOUT IT?
DO *YOU* KNOW WHO THIS NEW *MYSTERY HERO* IS?
NO, I DO *NOT,* MR. GOLD.

BUT I CAN *GUARANTEE* YOU I'M GOING TO *FIND OUT.*
C.KENT

RNNNG RNNNG
RNNNG RNNNG
...STEELWORKS...
HELLO, THIS IS KALA AVASTI CALLING FROM S.T.A.R. LABS. IS JOHN HENRY AVAILABLE?
HE'S OUT. I CAN TAKE A MESSAGE.
IF YOU WOULD, PLEASE. LET HIM KNOW THAT I'VE CONFIRMED THE TESTS, AND IT IS THE LUTHOR METAGENE STRAIN REWRITING HIS DNA.
...I'LL LET HIM KNOW...
I NEED HIM TO CALL ME AS SOON AS HE CAN.
UNCLE JOHN...
...YOU HYPOCRITE...
EXCORP Everyman Project
BE YOUR OWN HERO!

Week 8, Night 5

...AWW NO...

...NO, NO NO NO! C'MON!

...THIS ISN'T FAIR!
IT WAS ALMOST DONE!
NAT? YOU ALL RIGHT?

NO, I AM NOT ALL RIGHT!
I'VE BEEN WORKING ON THIS STUPID NEW SUIT FOR WEEKS AND WEEKS AND NOW IT'S TRASHED!
I'VE GOT METAL BURNS AND SLAG BURNS AND MY EYES HURT AND I'M TIRED AND IT'S ALL BECAUSE YOU WON'T LET ME HAVE MY OLD ARMOR!

BECAUSE YOU SAID I HADN'T EARNED IT--

--THAT I HAD TO MAKE IT MYSELF, THAT POWERS NEEDED TO BE EARNED AND NOT JUST GIVEN!
BUT I GUESS YOU ONLY MEANT ME, RIGHT?
NATASHA--

WHAT'S WITH THE SKIN, UNCLE JOHN? BROWN NOT GOOD ENOUGH FOR YOU--
DAMMIT, NAT--
DECIDED TO TRADE IT IN FOR SOMETHING MORE APPROPRIATE TO YOUR NAME?

SO DID YOU EARN IT, UNCLE JOHN?
DID YOU EARN THE POWERS LEX LUTHOR GAVE YOU?
YOU GONNA "BE YOUR OWN HERO"?

NATASHA, CALM DOWN. IT'S NOT WHAT YOU TH--
DON'T TALK TO ME--

--IT'S ALL LIES, ANYWAY, RIGHT?

I SHOULDN'T HAVE LISTENED TO YOU!
I SHOULD BE BACK THERE MAKING SURE THAT SHIP'S READY TO LAUNCH!
LISTEN, YOU WERE THE ONE WHO LET STARFIRE GO OFF ON HER OWN.

YOU GUYS SPENT WEEKS SPACED OUT ON ALIEN FRUIT!
ANIMAL MAN, I...
BUDDY.
I'M JUST SAYING, SHE'S BEEN GONE A LONG TIME.

IT'S A BIG PLANET.
SHE'S A WARRIOR PRINCESS, BUDDY, THINK ABOUT THOSE WORDS.
HAVE YOU EVER BEEN TO TAMARAN ?
NO...
WELL, I HAVE.

THESE ARE ADVANCED SOCIETIES. THE LIBERATION OF WOMEN MAY ONLY HAVE HAPPENED ON EARTH IN THE 1970s, BUT BELIEVE ME...
IT'S OLD NEWS EVERYWHERE ELSE IN THE SKY!

TRUST ME, SHE CAN TAKE CARE OF HERSELF.
ADAM, SHH!
I THINK I FOUND HER.

WHAT IS IT ?
IS SHE ALIVE ?
SOMEBODY STRUNG HER UP HERE, WHERE WE'D *FIND* HER.
LIKE *BAIT*.
ADAM, IT'S A *TRAP!*

--IN THE *PROPER* LINES!
THOSE OF YOU WHO HAVE *NOT* FILLED OUT *APPLICATIONS* NEED TO DO SO OR YOU WILL BE *DISQUALIFIED* FROM *CONSIDERATION!*
THOSE OF YOU WHO *HAVE* FILLED OUT APPLICATIONS BUT HAVE *NOT* SUBMITTED A *PROCESSING* FEE AND RECEIVED A *RECEIPT* WILL BE *DISQUALIFIED* FROM *CONSIDERATION!*
Week 8, Day 7
Metropolis.

THE *NEXT* BATCH OF CANDIDATES WILL BE *CHOSEN* AT THE *TOP* OF THE *HOUR...*
...ONCE *AGAIN,* YOU *MUST* REMAIN IN YOUR *LINES* OR YOU WILL BE *DISQUALIFIED!*
LUTHOR!
--ME! PICK ME, PLEASE--
LEX! LEX! MAKE ME *FLY,* THAT'S WHAT I WANT--
--ANYTHING I HAVE, *PLEASE*--
--SWEAR I'LL DO WHATEVER YOU WANT--

MR. LUTHOR!
LUTHOR!
PRESIDENT LUTHOR!
I LOVE YOU LEX!
LEX!
--LIKE THE *FLASH,* YOU KNOW, BEFORE HE *VANISHED*--
YOU KNOW WHAT *THEY* ARE, *MERCY?*
--TALL BUILDINGS IN A SINGLE *BOUND!*
SIR?

SLAVES.
AND THEY'RE ALL MINE...

TOLD ME TO STAND IN THIS LINE!
DON'T GET LIPPY WITH ME, GIRL, OR I'LL DISQUALIFY YOU HERE AND NOW!
SO WHAT AM I SUPPOSED TO DO? HUH?

WHAT SEEMS TO BE THE TROUBLE, LEWIS?
THIS... THIS YOUNG LADY DOESN'T HAVE A MINOR'S RELEASE, SIR, I WAS EXPLAINING--

IT'S NATASHA, ISN'T IT? NATASHA IRONS?
...YES, MISTER LUTHOR.
AND YOU'RE APPLYING FOR MY LITTLE PROGRAM, ARE YOU?
I WONDER WHAT YOUR UNCLE WOULD SAY ABOUT THAT.

MY UNCLE CAN GO TO HELL.

INDEED.

CONGRATULATIONS, NATASHA.
YOU'RE THE FIRST CANDIDATE OF THE DAY...

...NOW WHY DON'T YOU TELL ME WHO YOU REALLY WANT TO BE...

Week 8, Night 7
YOU'RE CERTAIN YOU WANT TO PROCEED WITHOUT THE REGULAR SCREENINGS?
DO I STRIKE YOU AS A MAN WHO SUFFERS DOUBT, DENNIS?
GET ON WITH IT. MAKE THE GIRL'S DREAM COME TRUE.
WHICH RESEQUENCING STRING, SIR?
THE WHOLE PACKAGE, DENNIS...
...SHE WANTS IT ALL...
...AND SHE WANTS IT NOW.
PROGRESS
SO LET'S GIVE IT TO HER.
PROGRESS
NEXT IN

WEEK EIGHT NOTES

GREG RUCKA

Pure Mark Waid gag on the third and fourth pages of the issue, and I laugh every time I read it. Maybe it's because I've got two kids and I've changed far too many diapers to count and I know just how expensive the disposables are, but I really want Ollie shooting a little higher.

Focus this issue is on the John Henry/ Natasha storyline, obviously, and this week sees the return of Doctor Kala Avasti and the continuation of John Henry's transformation into solid Steel. Thematically — at least in part — we're dealing with issues of transformation, clearly, and of responsibility and entitlement. John Henry's purpose, from the start, was to tell the story of the triumphant Everyman; in a year with Batman missing from the DCU, he was a logical self-made hero to take his place.

John Henry's refrain that rewards have to be earned, that hard work is required to attain them, and that strong personal responsibility is a prerequisite to putting on a costume, are all points that resonate very strongly with me. Contrasting his behavior this issue with the activities of the unseen Supernova (clearly a hero of whom John Henry would approve, a man who spots the problem, solves the problem, and then moves on to the next problem, not lingering for applause or accolades) and Booster's very visible, and — thank you, Clark Kent — well-documented tirades, makes this point all the more.

In fact, Booster is at the far end of a trajectory that Natasha starts upon in this issue, and (apparently) like Booster, it's one born out of impatience, entitlement, frustration, immaturity, and resentment. Add a dose of perceived betrayal (Q: Why did John Henry have an Everyman brochure in his briefcase? A: Because Lex Luthor is always up to something.) and a vicious slag burn to the cleavage, and you have teenage rebellion DCU style.

As a side note, the script called for Natasha to actually be wearing a welder's apron, so as to appear at least responsible enough not to forgo appropriate safety gear while working with molten metal. You can figure out all on your own why an artist or editor might decide not to go with that particular direction.

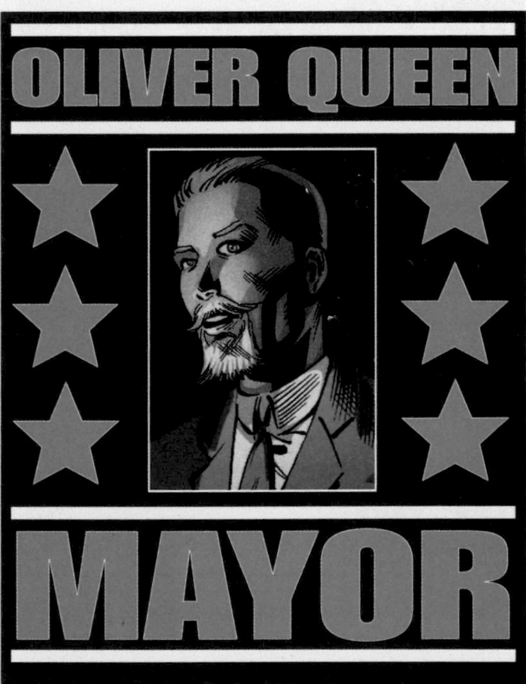

A peek into Oliver Queen's future.

(COMPARE WITH PAGE 202 OF THIS COLLECTION)

52 WEEK EIGHT — PAGE FOURTEEN

PANEL ONE
Angle, NATASHA in the Steelworks, still working on her ARMOR. She's hunched over a new metal plate, working a seam, the ACETYLENE TORCH roaring in her hands. GLOVES, MASK, APRON, SCARF...but the scarf has come loose, leaving a GAP at her neck and the front of the apron.

CAPTION: Week Eight, Night Five.

PANEL TWO
Tight, past the FLAME of the TORCH, welding METAL, to NATASHA, hunched over — it's damn hard to see with those masks on. The GAP from the SCARF should be clear, pretty much a straight shot to her upper chest/cleavage.

PANEL THREE
Same angle, but BOOM, the TORCH has hit a pocket of oxygen in the metal, and SPARKS of MOLTEN METAL are SHOWERING NATASHA. Most of them hit her protective gear, but of course several go right for the gap.

SFX: KSSHHH

NATASHA (muffled): Ow —

PANEL FOUR
NATASHA has jerked back, dropping the TORCH, which is immediately going out, and is yanking off her MASK with one hand, trying to unwrap her SCARF with the other. She's in serious pain, drops of molten metal burning her skin. In doing so, she's knocking the ARMOR from the table.

NATASHA: — ow ow OW dammit —

PANEL FIVE
On NATASHA, swiping her front, pulling the APRON away, cursing and wincing and generally being very unhappy with what just happened.

NATASHA: Dammit! Dammit! Stupid AIR pockets...

PANEL SIX
NATASHA, her expression changing, the pain and anger turning into absolute crestfallen despair.

NATASHA (small): ...aww no...

PANEL SEVEN
The ARMOR that she's been working on, now on the floor, broken apart. All of her welds have split. It looks like useless junk, that's what it looks like.

NATASHA (small/off-panel): ...no, no no no! C'mon!

PANEL EIGHT
On NATASHA, looking like she might not be able to keep from crying, holding a piece of her broken work.

NATASHA (small): ...this isn't FAIR! It was almost done!

JOHN HENRY (off-panel): Nat? You all RIGHT?

Metropolis.
Week 9 Day 1
THIS IS A COUNTRY FOUNDED ON A DREAM.
A DREAM OF EQUALITY AND OF EQUANIMITY. A DREAM OF PEACE AND OF HOPE, OF TOLERANCE AND PERSEVERANCE.
A DREAM WHERE EVERYONE-- EVEN A BOY FROM SMALLVILLE-- CAN BECOME, OH, I DON'T KNOW...
...PRESIDENT OF THE UNITED STATES?
HA HA HA
HA HA HA
HA HA HA
WE CALL IT THE AMERICAN DREAM.
BUT WHAT IS THAT, REALLY? A CHICKEN IN EVERY POT? A CAR IN EVERY GARAGE?
THAT WAS THE OLD DREAM, MY FRIENDS, MY GUESTS...
...I HAVE SEEN A NEW DREAM.
A DREAM WHERE EVERY MAN BECOMES A SUPER MAN.
GOD BLESS AMERICA.
GOD BLESS AMERICA!
DC COMICS 52

WRITTEN BY GEOFF JOHNS, GRANT MORRISON, GREG RUCKA, MARK WAID

ART BREAKDOWNS BY KEITH GIFFEN • PENCILS BY SHAWN MOLL • INKS BY TOM NGUYEN

COLORS BY DAVID BARON • LETTERING BY JARED K. FLETCHER

LET HIM GO!
BLAM
BLAM

YOU THINK THAT'S GOING TO WORK?
DIDN'T YOUR BOSS TELL YOU WHAT HE WAS GOING TO DO TO ME--

HOW HE WAS GOING TO CHANGE ME--
MAKE ME MATCH MY NAME?

AAAHH!

I WANT MY NIECE BACK. IF YOU'VE SO MUCH AS TOUCHED HER, LEX--
I'VE DONE MUCH MORE THAN THAT, JOHN...
...I'VE MADE HER DREAMS COME TRUE...
NNH

...WHICH IS FAR MORE THAN YOU'VE EVER DONE, I THINK YOU'LL AGREE.
YOU NEVER CHANGE. ALWAYS TAKING WHAT'S NOT YOURS TO TAKE...

...GIVING WHAT'S NOT YOURS TO GIVE.
LAST CHANCE:
WHERE IS SHE?
SHE'S RIGHT HERE.

AND SHE THINKS YOU BETTER PUT HER BOSS DOWN...
...BEFORE YOU GET HURT.

HUFF
UNDO IT!
CHANGE HER BACK!
LET HIM GO, JOHN!

YOU BASTARD, I'LL KILL YOU--
NO--

NFFF
LEAVE HIM ALONE!

YOU PICKED THE WRONG GROUP, OLD MAN--
NO! HERAKLES!
GET BACK...

...LET ME HANDLE HIM....

DON'T FIGHT ME, UNCLE JOHN!
KRRKKKSHH
WHAT HAPPENED TO YOU, NAT?
DIDN'T YOU HEAR A THING I SAID TO YOU?
I HEARD IT ALL! BUT THE WORLD DOESN'T WORK LIKE YOU WANT IT TO WORK!
THE WORLD DOESN'T CARE HOW MUCH YOU WORK OR HOW HARD YOU TRY!
LOOK AT YOU! LOOK AT WHAT HAPPENED TO YOU! LOOK AT MY PARENTS! WHERE ARE THEY NOW, HUH?
YOU TAKE WHAT YOU CAN, WHEN YOU CAN!
ONLY A FOOL WOULD DO ANYTHING ELSE.

YOU'VE GOT NO IDEA WHAT I'VE BECOME!
YOU'LL LOSE, DON'T YOU UNDERSTAND?
YOU HAVE NO IDEA HOW POWERFUL LUTHOR'S MADE ME!
WHOOM
THEN I GUESS I'M A FOOL...
...BECAUSE I CANNOT LET YOU DO THIS.
NOT TO YOURSELF, AND NOT FOR A MAN LIKE LEX LUTHOR.
YOU CAN'T STOP ME!
THIS IS BETWEEN LEX AND ME! GET OUT OF THE WAY, NATASHA!
MAKE ME.

WHAM
GNNHH!

KERRASH

--STAND DOWN, UNCLE JOHN!
YOU'VE ALREADY LOST!
UNNF

...NO...
...THAT MAN'S TAKEN TOO MUCH FROM ME--

--HE CAN'T HAVE YOU, TOO!

GET OUT OF THE WAY!

NOW DO YOU GET IT?
NOW ARE YOU BEGINNING TO SEE?
SZZZ

THIS IS WHAT I'VE ALWAYS WANTED, TO BECOME THE HERO YOU'RE ALWAYS TALKING ABOUT...
...TO HAVE THE POWER TO DO IT.

IF YOU'D HIT LUTHOR WITH THAT, HE'D BE DEAD NOW, UNCLE JOHN...
...YOU'D HAVE MURDERED HIM.

SO YOU TELL ME...
...WHICH OF US IS THE HERO, HERE?
NO!

YOU'RE CONFUSED, NAT, YOU'RE NOT THINKING STRAIGHT--
IT'S YOU WHO'S LOST HIS MIND...

...NOT ME!

YOU'RE RIGHT.
BUT I'M RIGHT, TOO.
NATASHA... PLEASE...

...GIVE IT UP, COME HOME...

UNCLE JOHN...

...HAVEN'T YOU HEARD ANYTHING I'VE SAID?
THIS IS WHAT I WANT--
NHN!

--I'LL *NEVER* GIVE IT UP--
FWAM

NOT FOR *YOU*--
--NOT FOR *ANYONE!*
NNNGHH...

GHNNHHH!
WHAM

THERE'S HEAT ON MY FACE THAT FEELS LIKE THE SUN.
LIKE A DOZEN TINY SUNS.
THE FIRST THING I THINK ABOUT WHEN I WAKE UP AGAIN IS MY WIFE.
THEN THE KIDS.
I HOPE THE WORLD MADE IT.
I'M ON AN ALIEN PLANET LIGHT-YEARS FROM HOME, TRUSSED UP WITH A COUPLE OF SPACE HEROES CALLED STARFIRE AND ADAM STRANGE.
THE GIANT WHO TRAPPED US LIKE ANIMALS HAS BEEN KEEPING US HERE FOR DAYS.
I THINK HE'S GOING TO EAT US.
HE CALLS HIMSELF DEVILANCE THE PURSUER.

OKAY, I HAVE A PLAN...

HE COULDN'T CUT ME OFF FROM THE SOURCE OF MY POWER.

ANIMAL LIFE.

GGAAAUU!

COVER ME, BUDDY!

CLOSE YOUR EYES!

TOO BAD FOR HIM.

YOU SNEAKED UP ON ME THE LAST TIME.

LET'S SEE HOW YOU LIKE A FAIR FIGHT.

...WELL, YOU SAID WE NEEDED A POWER SOURCE, ADAM.
HOW ABOUT THIS?
THAT LANCE... THAT'S OUR WAY OFF THIS PLANET.
SEE?
I TOLD YOU I'D SORT SOMETHING OUT.

YEAH, BUT WHAT WAS HE TALKING ABOUT?
ALL THAT "WALLS OF HEAVEN" STUFF?
WHAT DID IT SOUND LIKE?
IT MEANS HE'S NOT THE ONLY ONE.
SOMEONE THINKS WE SAW SOMETHING HUMANS WEREN'T MEANT TO SEE, AND HE TOLD ME THEY'VE PUT OUT A CONTRACT ON US.

EVEN IF WE MAKE IT OFF-WORLD, WE'RE GOING TO HAVE EVERY BOUNTY HUNTER IN THE KNOWN UNIVERSE ON OUR TAILS.

GREAT.
I'LL JUST CARRY THIS BACK THEN, SHALL I?
THAT'S WHAT I LOVE ABOUT BEING A SUPERHERO...

THE ENDLESS COMPLICATIONS.

Gotham City.
...THAT WAS A NICE ONE...
...LIKE THE GREEN ONES...
...ANOTHER BEER, I'M GETTING ONE...
Week 9, Night 1

HEY, BUDDY, YOU LOST?
YOU LOOK LIKE YOU WANT DIXIELAND, THAT'S THE NEXT BLOCK.

YOU THINK?
MOLLY'S

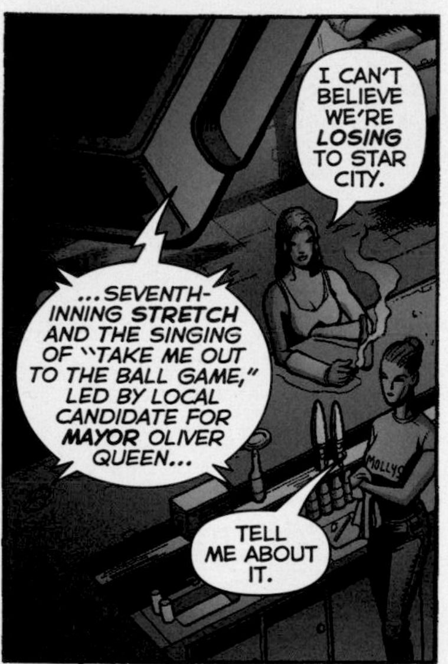
I CAN'T BELIEVE WE'RE LOSING TO STAR CITY.
...SEVENTH-INNING STRETCH AND THE SINGING OF "TAKE ME OUT TO THE BALL GAME," LED BY LOCAL CANDIDATE FOR MAYOR OLIVER QUEEN...
TELL ME ABOUT IT.

AT LEAST WE'RE KICKING METROPOLIS'S ASS THIS YEAR.
CAN I HELP YOU?

BOTTLE OF LIT, PLEASE.
...OOO-KAY...

WHAT INNING?
SEVENTH, STARS FIVE, KNIGHTS TWO.
YOU KNOW THIS IS A LESBIAN BAR, RIGHT?

SO NO MEN'S ROOM, HUH?
SMART-ASS.

CONSISTENCY IS EVERYTHING.
BY THE WAY...
...HOW'S YOUR ARM?

WHO ARE YOU?
NO, I ASKED YOU FIRST, AND I'M STILL WAITING FOR AN ANSWER.

YOU.

ME.

I WAS WONDERING IF I'D EVER SEE YOUR FACE AGAIN.
ONE OF THEM, ANYWAY.

MY NAME'S VIC, BUT MY FRIENDS CALL ME CHARLIE.

CURIOUS?
FULL OF QUESTIONS?
C'MON...

...I MIGHT HAVE SOME ANSWERS FOR YOU...

I'M WONDERING WHY I SHOULDN'T BEAT YOU WITHIN AN INCH OF YOUR LIFE, CHARLIE.
YOU HAVE IMPULSE CONTROL ISSUES, DON'T YOU?
I THOUGHT YOU WERE GONE FOR GOOD!

HEY, I GOT HURT IN THAT FIGHT, TOO, YOU KNOW.
SO, YOU GONNA TELL ME WHAT YOU'VE LEARNED?
YOUR MONEY RAN OUT A MONTH AGO, SMART-GUY!
WHAT MAKES YOU THINK I'M EVEN STILL INTERESTED IN YOUR LITTLE MYSTERY?

BECAUSE YOU'RE LIKE ME.
YOU'RE CURIOUS.

YOU ALMOST GOT ME KILLED! MY CURIOSITY DOESN'T EXTEND THAT FAR!
SURE IT DOES. WHY ELSE ARE YOU STILL LOOKING INTO IT?

WAIT--YOU'VE BEEN SPYING ON ME?
I WANTED TO MAKE SURE YOU WERE ALL RIGHT.

WHO ARE YOU?
I MEAN, JUST WHO THE HELL ARE YOU?

LIKE I KEEP SAYING...

...I ASKED YOU FIRST...
FSSSS

NEAT TRICK.
HOW... HOW'S IT WORK?
SEE? QUESTIONS, THAT'S GOOD, THAT'S WHY I LIKE YOU.
THE CLOTHES AND THE MASK ARE CHEMICALLY TREATED, ACTIVATED BY THE BINARY GAS RELEASED FROM THE BELT BUCKLE.

WHY SHOW ME THAT?
TO PROVE A COUPLE POINTS.
FIRST, THAT I TRUST YOU.

SECOND, THAT MOST ANSWERS LEAD TO MORE QUESTIONS.
HOW MANY MORE DO YOU HAVE NOW, RENEE?
OH, ANOTHER TWO DOZEN OR SO...
...BUT MOSTLY I KEEP COMING BACK TO THE SAME ONES.
WHAT THE HELL'S GOING ON? WHAT WAS THAT THING THAT ATTACKED US? WHAT WERE THOSE WEAPONS? WHERE'D THEY COME FROM?

GOTHAM IS BEING TARGETED, RENEE.
WHAT WE FOUND WAS THE GROUNDWORK FOR AN INVASION...

...GOTHAM CITY IS BEING TARGETED BY INTERGANG.

NEXT IN 52

WEEK NINE NOTES

KEITH GIFFEN

I'll admit it. It was me. I designed the initial Infinity Inc. costumes. In hindsight... euww. Thank God they went with someone else for the Batwoman design. Speaking of Batwoman, this issue became the character's inadvertent reveal. In the breakdowns, I'd dropped the Batwoman figure in the final panel into silhouette, figuring her big reveal would play out down the line. Somehow wires got crossed and there she was for all to see. Best laid plans...

Leave it to Grant to bump 52 up against the New Gods mythos and make it work. Devilance came as a complete surprise to me, a pleasant surprise since this obscure New God was one of my favorites. Nine issues in and I could still be taken by surprise. That felt good. Not good enough to completely overcome my "will we pull this off" concerns, but close.

About those concerns. I was foolish enough to think that, once we got further in, once we had a big ol' stack of completed issues inventoried and ready to go, that those concerns would go away. They never went away. Up until the final issue, they never went away. It wasn't because I thought that one of the creative team would fumble the ball or feared that a print run would go awry — it's just the way I'm wired.

Hell, I'm concerned that this trade won't make it out on time...

Batwoman turnaround by **Alex Ross**

SKETCHES

Fan-favorite artist **Alex Ross** went through numerous Batwoman head designs before the final version was chosen.

Kahndaq.

Week 10, Day 1

<I CANNOT CHANGE THE WORLD ALONE.>

<WHICH IS WHY I'VE CALLED KAHNDAQ'S ALLIES HERE.>

<WE WILL DO OUR BEST TO MAKE THEM FEEL WELCOME.>

<I'M SURE YOU WILL.>

SHAZAM.

Hhn.

STOP THE PRESS
WRITTEN BY GEOFF JOHNS, GRANT MORRISON, GREG RUCKA, MARK WAID
ART BREAKDOWNS BY KEITH GIFFEN • PENCILS BY CHRIS BATISTA • INKS BY JIMMY PALMIOTTI & JACK JADSON
COLORS BY ALEX SINCLAIR • LETTERING BY JARED K. FLETCHER • COVER BY J.G. JONES & ALEX SINCLAIR
ASSISTANT EDITORS JANN JONES & HARVEY RICHARDS
EDITED BY STEPHEN WACKER
SPECIAL THANKS TO IVAN COHEN

<EACH ONE OF YOU IS A REPRESENTATIVE FOR YOUR GREAT COUNTRY, AND I ASK EACH ONE OF YOU TO DELIVER A MESSAGE TO YOUR LEADERS.>
<MANY HAVE JOINED OUR COALITION, BUT MANY MORE HAVE BEEN RESISTANT... SOME OF YOU HAVE BEEN RESISTANT TO ALLOW OTHERS IN...>
<...BUT THAT WILL CHANGE. AS OF NOW, I ASK YOU TO FORGET THE POLITICAL BATTLES BETWEEN ONE ANOTHER.>
<ALREADY CHINA AND RUSSIA HAVE AGREED TO CREATE A CLEAN SLATE WITH MYSELF AS THE MODERATOR.>
<SOON, WE WILL HAVE THE STRENGTH TO-->
<STOP!>

<STOP!>

<STOP HER!>

<LET ME GO!>

<WE ARE SORRY FOR THE INTERRUPTION. SHE THREW HER DINNER IN MAQUED'S FACE AND RAN.>
<A THOUSAND APOLOGIES, MIGHTY ADAM.>
<WHAT IS WRONG WITH THE GIRL?>

<MY *NAME* IS ADRIANNA TOMAZ.>
<AND *YOU* ARE NOTHING BUT A *TERRORIST.*>

NOT WISE...

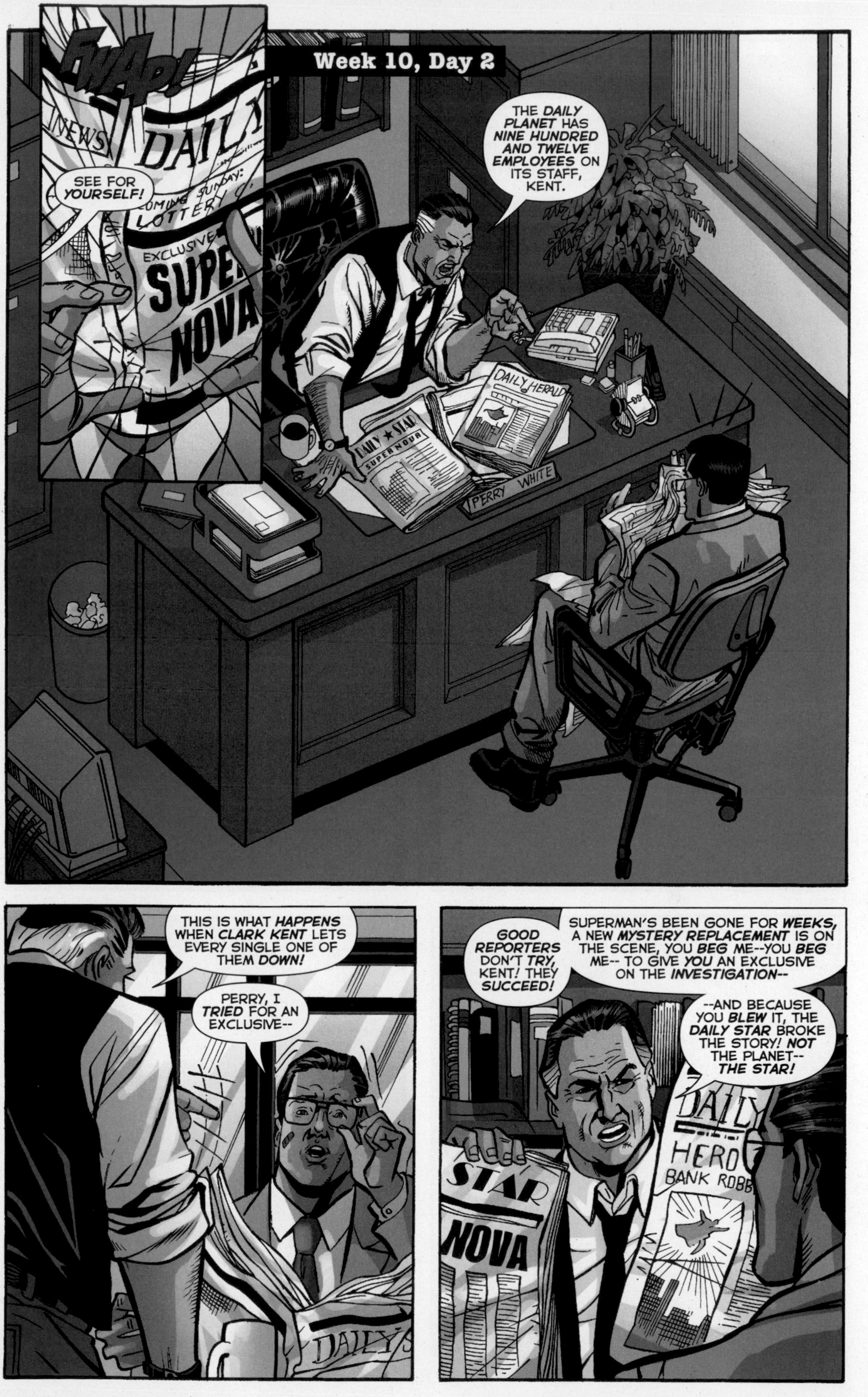

Week 10, Day 2

FWAP!

SEE FOR *YOURSELF!*

THE *DAILY PLANET* HAS *NINE HUNDRED AND TWELVE EMPLOYEES* ON ITS STAFF, KENT.

THIS IS WHAT *HAPPENS* WHEN *CLARK KENT* LETS EVERY SINGLE ONE OF THEM *DOWN!*
PERRY, I *TRIED* FOR AN EXCLUSIVE--

SUPERMAN'S BEEN GONE FOR *WEEKS,* A NEW *MYSTERY REPLACEMENT* IS ON THE SCENE, YOU *BEG* ME--YOU *BEG* ME-- TO GIVE *YOU* AN EXCLUSIVE ON THE *INVESTIGATION--*
GOOD REPORTERS DON'T *TRY,* KENT! THEY *SUCCEED!*
--AND BECAUSE YOU *BLEW* IT, THE *DAILY STAR* BROKE THE STORY! *NOT* THE PLANET-- *THE STAR!*
STAR
NOVA
HERO
BANK ROBB

TO ADD INSULT TO INJURY, THE STAR LAID CLAIM TO HIM BY NAMING THE DAMN GUY "SUPERNOVA!"
MEANWHILE, "REPORTER" CLARK KENT IS SIX STEPS BEHIND THE PONY EXPRESS ON THIS AND WHAT IS WRONG WITH YOUR FACE?
I CUT MYSELF SHAVING.

AGAIN? IF YOU DON'T KNOW HOW TO USE A KEYBOARD, KENT, TELL ME YOU AT LEAST KNOW HOW TO USE A RAZOR!
KIND OF.
DON'T GET CUTE! I'M NOT JOKING HERE! THIS ISN'T CUDDLY PERRY BLOWING OFF STEAM! KENT...

...CLARK...
...I'M... I'M...

Notice of Termination

YOU'RE FIRING ME?

IT'S NOT JUST THIS, CLARK. IT'S EVERYTHING ELSE YOU'VE LET SLIDE SO FAR THIS YEAR. BIG THINGS.
MR. WHITE, I ADMIT I'VE BEEN IN A SLUMP--
IN THIS BUSINESS, KENT, TWO WEEKS IS A SLUMP. FOUR WEEKS IS BURNOUT.

AFTER SEVEN WEEKS OF WATCHING YOU WALK AROUND LIKE YOU'VE FORGOTTEN EVERYTHING YOU KNOW ABOUT REPORTING, I WENT AGAINST MY EVERY INSTINCT--
--AND GAVE THE SUPERNOVA ASSIGNMENT TO YOU, PRAYING TO GOD ABOVE THAT YOU COULD DELIVER IN A TIMELY FASHION.
MR. WHITE, I CAN DO BETTER--

NO KIDDING! THAT'S THE POINT, KENT!

I DON'T KNOW WHAT SECRET SKILLS AND TRICKS YOU'VE BEEN RELYING ON ALL THESE YEARS AS AN INVESTIGATIVE REPORTER.

WORSE, I DON'T KNOW WHERE THEY WENT.
BUT ONCE THEY WENT, IT BECAME APPARENT TO ME THAT, A LOT OF TIMES, YOU LET STORIES FALL INTO YOUR LAP RATHER THAN FIGHT FOR THEM.

YOU USED TO BE GREAT, KENT. YOU USED TO TAKE RISKS. YOU USED TO PUT YOURSELF IN THE THICK OF NEWS.

NOW YOU KEEP YOUR DISTANCE. AND THAT'S NOT THE JOB.

SO I'M FIRED.
YOU COST US A LOT OF CREDIBILITY, CLARK.

SO FAR, THIS SUPERNOVA IS STILL JUST A HEADLINE AND A PHOTO.

THERE'S STILL TIME FOR THE PLANET TO GET THE FIRST REAL INTERVIEW--
--BUT IT WON'T BE BY YOU. I'VE REASSIGNED IT TO TROUPE. HE'LL GET IT SOMEHOW.

YOU NEVER TOLD ME THIS WAS MY LAST CHANCE, MR. WHITE.
I'M SORRY, KENT, BUT--
GREAT CAESAR'S GHOST, KENT, WHAT ARE YOU DOING?

KENT, WAIT! IT'S NOT WORTH KILLING YOURSELF, MAN!

KENT!

EASY, MISTER. I'VE GOT YOU. ARE YOU OKAY?
I'M FINE. CLARK KENT, DAILY PLANET.
LET'S TALK...

<WE HAD BETTER HAVE NO MORE TROUBLE FROM *YOU,* OR IT'S ANOTHER 24 HOURS IN THE HOLDING CELL.>
NNFF

<THERE ARE WORSE QUARTERS TO BE IN THAN *THIS* ROOM.>

<ENOUGH.>
<BUT, ADAM-->
<LEAVE US.>

<WHY WERE YOU RUNNING?>

<I WON'T BE A PRISONER.>
<PRISONER? YOU ARE NOT A PRISONER.>
<YOU ARE A REFUGEE.>

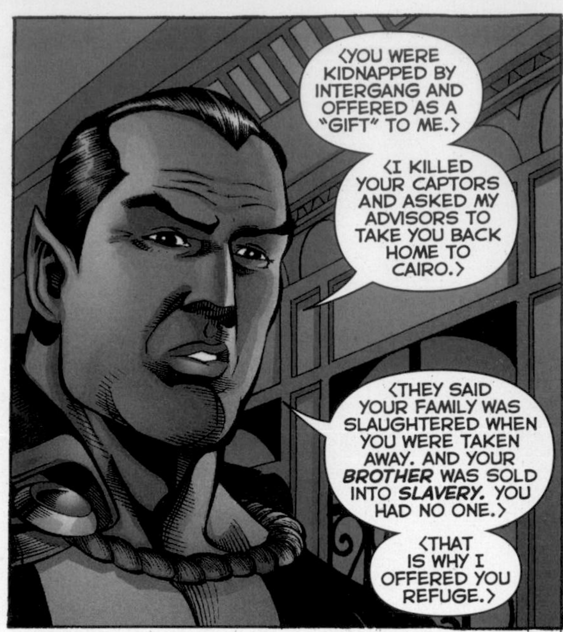

<YOU WERE KIDNAPPED BY INTERGANG AND OFFERED AS A "GIFT" TO ME.>
<I KILLED YOUR CAPTORS AND ASKED MY ADVISORS TO TAKE YOU BACK HOME TO CAIRO.>
<THEY SAID YOUR FAMILY WAS SLAUGHTERED WHEN YOU WERE TAKEN AWAY. AND YOUR BROTHER WAS SOLD INTO SLAVERY. YOU HAD NO ONE.>
<THAT IS WHY I OFFERED YOU REFUGE.>

<I APOLOGIZE...>
<...FOR KILLING YOUR CAPTORS AND DENYING YOU YOUR REVENGE.>
<YOU APOLOGIZE FOR THAT?>

<YOU'RE FREE TO LEAVE AT ANY...>

<...TIME.>

<YOU'RE NOT GOING TO CHANGE THE WORLD.>

<EXCUSE ME?>
<THESE LAST SEVERAL WEEKS, I'VE SEEN AND HEARD ABOUT THIS *CRUSADE* OF YOURS.>
<IT BORDERS ON *PSYCHOTIC.*>
<REALLY?>

<YOU'RE GATHERING A COALITION OF OTHER COUNTRIES THAT WILL ADOPT YOUR *FREEDOM OF POWER TREATY.*>
<EFFECTIVELY ENFORCING LETHAL ACTION AGAINST META-HUMAN CRIMINALS.>

<SOME OF THEM HAVE THE POWER TO DESTROY A COUNTRY. IF THEY HAVE THE INCLINATION, THEY MUST BE *DISMANTLED.*>
<YOU'RE TARGETING AMERICA.>
<YOU'RE HOPING TO CONCENTRATE A POWER BASE TO RIVAL *THEIRS.*>
<I'M SIMPLY SPREADING A METHOD OF *JUSTICE* THAT WILL HELP PROTECT THE PEOPLE AND INSURE THAT NO ONE WILL AGAIN LOSE THEIR FAMILY AS YOU HAVE *YOURS.*>

<YOU'RE GOING TO PLUNGE THIS WORLD INTO *WAR.*>
<WHAT *HAPPENED* TO YOU?>
<WHAT HAPPENED THAT YOU TAKE IT OUT ON THE WHOLE WORLD?>

<YOU ARE FREE TO GO NOW.>

<YOUR PROBLEM IS THAT YOU DON'T LISTEN TO ANYONE BUT YOURSELF.>
<AND YOUR PROBLEM IS THAT YOU ARE *NAIVE.*>
<*ARROGANT.*>
<*DISRESPECTFUL.*>

<*ALONE.*>

Week 10, Day 3

YOU DID WHAT?
FWAP!
DAILY PLANET
SUPERNOVA
EXCLUSIVE

WHAT EVER POSSESSED YOU TO THROW YOURSELF OUT A WINDOW TO GET SOMEONE'S ATTENTION?
THE MEMORY OF YOU ASKING ME THAT WITH A STRAIGHT FACE WILL LAST A LIFETIME.
LOIS, YOU. WROTE THE PLAYBOOK ON THIS.

LOOK AROUND YOU, CLARK. THIS IS A WHOLE NEW BALL GAME.
ACCORDING TO THE MEDIA, THE PUBLIC IS REELING FROM "POST-CRISIS TRAUMA."

BIG SUPER-HERO/ SUPER-VILLAIN BRAWLS, THOSE WE TAKE FOR GRANTED. BUT WE MERE MORTALS AREN'T ACCUSTOMED TO THE THREAT OF TOTAL ARMAGEDDON.
YES, BY THE SKIN OF YOUR GLEAMING WHITE TEETH, YOU GUYS SAVED THE EARTH-- BUT YOU WEREN'T ABLE TO PUT IT BACK EXACTLY AS IT WAS. PEOPLE ARE STILL, HOW YOU SAY, FREAKED.
JOURNAL
JULY
WHERE IS THE JLA?!

THIS IS A WORLD WITHOUT WONDER WOMAN AND FLASH. WHERE'D THEY GO?
ALL I'M TOLD IS THAT THEY'RE SAFE.
BATMAN AND ROBIN?
OFF THE RECORD? TRAVELING THE GLOBE TO REBUILD THEIR SKILLS.
AND SUPERMA--

--SWEETIE, HOT!
RIGHT. THANKS.

--SUPERMAN'S ABSENCE IS KEENLY FELT.
I'LL BE BACK. IT'S... JUST TAKING A WHILE TO RECHARGE.

OKAY, YOU KNOW THAT I DON'T CARE, RIGHT? THAT I MARRIED THE MAN AND NOT THE CAPE.

WE'VE DISCUSSED THIS. I'M NOT WORRIED ABOUT IT.

I'LL BE BACK. BUT UNTIL I AM, THIS JUST MIGHT BE SUPERNOVA'S TOWN.
TELL ME, MR. REHIRED-WITH-A-RAISE--

"OKAY. REMEMBER HOW THERE'D BEEN A RUMOR ALL MORNING THAT BAHDNESIAN TERRORISTS WERE OUT TO STEAL THE ARMY'S NEW MORTARPROOF ALL-TERRAIN?
"BEFORE I COULD FIRE OFF MY FIRST QUESTION, WE'D SPOTTED THEM TEARING UP MEMORIAL DRIVE.

"A SECOND LATER, I BECAME THE LATEST EYEWITNESS--

"--AS SUPERNOVA FIRED OFF A PECULIAR EYEBEAM THAT TOOK OUT A CHUNK OF PAVEMENT.

"LITERALLY, TOOK OUT. VANISHED? DISINTEGRATED? NOT EVEN THE CAMERA COULD TELL FOR CERTAIN--"

"--BUT HE DEFINITELY SHOWED THE TERRORISTS THAT ALL-TERRAIN IS NOT THE SAME AS NO-TERRAIN.

"I'D GOTTEN THE FIRST CLEAR PHOTOS OF SUPERNOVA-- AND THE FIRST INTERVIEW. HE WAS GUARDED--
"--DIDN'T SAY ANYTHING ESPECIALLY REVELATORY, A LOT OF THE STANDARD 'I'M HERE TO HELP' LANGUAGE--"
THAT KID--

"--BUT HE MADE A VERY CLASSY EXIT."
HE'S NOT WATCHING WHERE HE'S GOING...!

STAY BACK, PAL! THAT'S AN AWFULLY DEEP HOLE IN THE PAVEMENT!
"LIKE I TOLD PERRY... I THINK HE'S ON THE LEVEL."

YOU'RE SURE? YOU TEND TO BE VERY... GENEROUS WITH THE BENEFIT OF THE DOUBT, HONEY.
HE HAS AN AIR OF EXPERIENCE TO HIM. WOULD YOU HAVE THOUGHT THAT QUICKLY TO SECURE THE CRIME SCENE OR PROTECT BYSTANDERS?
EITHER WAY, THE QUESTION REMAINS...

...WHO'S UNDERNEATH THAT *MASK?*

Week 10, Day 4

IT'S A MYSTERY TO *ME,* SIR.

YEAH? Y'KNOW WHAT *ELSE* IS A MYSTERY? HOW I'M GONNA ADJUST FROM LIVING IN A *PENTHOUSE* CONDO TO A %&$#@@-$#@$&%! THREE-ROOM *RENTAL* WITH AN *ALLEY VIEW--*

...MY CONTACTS IN THE MILITARY FINALLY SECURED ME PRIVILEGED ACCESS TO THE CONTENTS OF DOCTOR SIVANA'S LABORATORY.
Week 10, Day 6

I SALVAGED A "SIVANIUM" ROBOT HE'D BEEN WORKING ON BEFORE HE WAS ABDUCTED.
I THOUGHT MAYBE I COULD REHABILITATE THE THING BUT... WELL, IF YOU CAN IMAGINE A LIVING METAL WITH SIVANA'S OBNOXIOUS PERSONALITY...
OTHERWISE, IT WAS ALL WEIRD, CRANKY STUFF NOBODY KNEW WHAT TO DO WITH...

SO... WHAT DID YOU FIND, WILL?
I'M NOT SURE.
I WAS SURPRISED THEY LET ME TAKE WHAT I DID.
I THOUGHT THEY HATED ME.

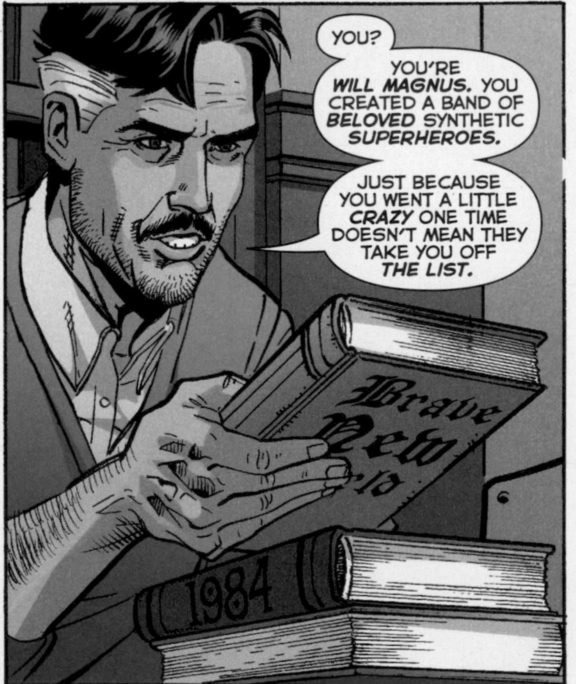
YOU?
YOU'RE WILL MAGNUS. YOU CREATED A BAND OF BELOVED SYNTHETIC SUPERHEROES.
JUST BECAUSE YOU WENT A LITTLE CRAZY ONE TIME DOESN'T MEAN THEY TAKE YOU OFF THE LIST.
Brave New
1984

WE ALL GO A LITTLE CRAZY SOMETIMES.
OF COURSE... SOME OF US GET LOCKED UP FOR IT.
FRANKENSTEIN

STILL...MUSN'T COMPLAIN.
WE MARCH TO A DIFFERENT DRUM, YOU AND I. HISTORY WILL JUDGE US, NOT LAW.
WHAT ARE YOU TRYING TO SAY, PROFESSOR MORROW ?

JUST...
THANK YOU, WILL.
THANK YOU FOR BEING MY FRIEND.

YOU'RE TALKING LIKE WE'RE NEVER GOING TO SEE ONE ANOTHER AGAIN.
IS THERE SOMETHING YOU HAVEN'T TOLD ME?

WALLS HAVE EARS, WILL.
NOW SHOW ME WHAT YOU FOUND.
WHAT WAS MAD DOCTOR SIVANA UP TO?
HOW ABOUT THIS, INSIDE A BROKEN GLASS JAR?
HE'D BEEN TREATING IT WITH RADIATION.
IT... AH... IT SEEMS TO BE A COCOON OF SOME KIND.
HNN.
NOW WHAT DO YOU SUPPOSE HATCHED OUT OF THERE...?
NEXT IN 52

WEEK TEN NOTES

GREG RUCKA

You just know it's gonna be love when Andrea spits in Black Adam's face and lives to tell the tale.

The Clark/Perry sequence at the *Daily Planet* is, incidentally, one of my most favorite moments in all of the 52 issues, and was entirely conceived of and written by Mark Waid. I think it is a masterly bit of storytelling, personally — in one elegant sequence, we see Clark not only grappling with his loss of powers, but we see the core courage and audacity that truly makes him Superman, those missing powers notwithstanding. How many times has Clark gone out the window without a second's thought? And here, he does it again, gambling that Supernova will catch him in time. That, ladies and gentlemen, is called stones, and that — as much as being able to fly and fire heat rays from his eyes — makes Clark Kent Superman. The final touch, of course, is that our currently-in-forced-retirement Superman is rescued from certain death by his apparent heir.

There was a nice bit of serendipity in this issue, as well — the major action consisting of one-on-one scenes throughout. Black Adam and Andrea laying the seeds of their romance contrasting with Lois and Clark's enduring affection. Skeets and Booster, even Morrow and Magnus. While the issue itself serves, in the main, to promote the "Who is Supernova?" mystery (and to a lesser extent the "what happened to the missing scientists and, while we're at it, where the hell did Mister Mind go?"), at the same time it establishes and reinforces some of the most crucial relationships to the overall story of *52*. As it's those relationships that are the driving force in the remaining 42 weeks, the continued expansion of them is crucial.

OFFICIAL SUPERNOVA CUT-OUT MASK INSTRUCTIONS

1. Tear out mask on reverse side and glue page to cardstock.
2. Carefully cut out mask along dotted line using scissors. (Kids — ask a parent for help!).
3. Use scissors to also cut out eye holes (nostril holes are optional).
4. With a hole puncher, punch out holes at either side of the mask.
5. Cut two pieces of string (approx. 6 in.), and tie or tape each piece into the punched holes.
6. Tie the ends of the strings together in the back of your head.
7. Confound your friends with the mystery of "Who is Supernova?"

Week 11, Night 5
Washington, DC
COOL.
ACCEPTED.
NOOBS MEETIN' TOMORROW NIGHT, IF YOU WANNA CHECK IT OUT. GOOD PLACE TO HANG--

WHERE IS HE?
AAHHHHH!

AAHHHHH!
ANSWER ME!

EVERY DAMN DAY, HIS "CULT OF CONNER" PULLS IN KIDS ALL OVER THE COUNTRY!
IF YOU'RE A MEMBER, YOU KNOW WHERE TO FIND THEM, AND YOU ARE GOING TO TELL ME--

--BECAUSE I AM FLAT OUT OF PATIENCE!
AHUH AHUH AHUH AHUH AHUH

SEE *THIS?* THIS MAN'S *ACOLYTES* DESECRATED MY WIFE'S *GRAVE!* THEY PLAYED ME FOR A *FOOL!*
THEY STOLE MY *WEDDING RING!*

CULT OF CONNER

NOW THEY'RE *EVERYWHERE* AND *NOWHERE* AT THE *SAME TIME!* EVERY TIME I THINK I'VE CAUGHT *UP* TO THEM, THEY'RE *GONE--* SO *YOU TELL ME WHERE...*

DON'T HURT ME *DON'T HURT ME* DON'T--

...WHERE...

...OH, MY GOD...HOW *OLD* ARE YOU...?

OFFA HER!

WHACK

WAIT... I'M *SORRY...*

...I DIDN'T REALIZE...

bdeep bdeep

PLEASE BE BEA...PLEASE BE *BEA...*

HELLO?

SIGH

RALPH DIBNY? THIS IS BERNIE OUT AT OPAL CITY STORAGE.

SIR, THAT UNIT YOU RENTED?

WRITTEN BY GEOFF JOHNS, GRANT MORRISON, GREG RUCKA, MARK WAID
BREAKDOWNS BY KEITH GIFFEN

ART BY JOE BENNETT, TODD NAUCK, JACK JADSON & MARLO ALQUIZA

Here it comes.
YOU REALLY SHOULD QUIT.
GUARDIAN CIGARETTES
Gotham City.
Week 11, Day 6

Like a broken record.
LET ME GUESS, YOU USED TO SMOKE.
THERE'S HYDROGEN CYANIDE IN CIGARETTE SMOKE, RENEE.
THAT'S THE STUFF THE NAZIS USED TO MURDER THE JEWS IN THE GAS CHAMBERS...

COLORS BY ALEX SINCLAIR • LETTERING BY NICK J. NAPOLITANO
ASSISTANT EDITORS JANN JONES & HARVEY RICHARDS

EDITED BY STEPHEN WACKER COVER BY J.G. JONES & SINCLAIR

...and the *reopening* of some very *old* wounds.
HUBBA-HUBBA.
SHUT.
UP.
This particular old wound has a name.

Billionaire heiress and drop-dead knockout Kate Kane.
THANKS FOR COMING, KATE.
RENEE.

I was in love with her once.
WHO'S YOUR *FRIEND?*
I'M HER *PARTNER*, CHARLIE. PLEASED TO *MEET* YOU, MS. KANE.
WHO'S *YOURS?*

HER NAME'S MALLORY, SHE'S A *DOCTOR.*
I tell *myself* *I'm* not anymore.
GOTHAM GAZETTE

It *shouldn't* bother me.
YOU *DON'T* KNOW HER.
It *does* anyway.

It *doesn't* matter. It's not why she's here.
WHAT DO YOU *HAVE* FOR ME?

She's here because the Kane family has more money than God, and much of it is in Gotham City real estate.
YOU WERE CORRECT, THE FAMILY DOES OWN THE PROPERTY AT FIVE-TWENTY KANE STREET.
LIKE MOST OF OUR HOLDINGS, IT'S CONTROLLED THROUGH ONE OF SEVERAL MANAGEMENT COMPANIES...

Six weeks ago Charlie and I got our clocks cleaned at five-twenty Kane Street.
...WE HAVE NO DIRECT INVOLVEMENT--
THANKS.

The thing that cleaned our clocks wasn't what I'd call human.
IS IT CURRENTLY BEING RENTED?
The thing that cleaned our clocks got turned to a puff of vapor.

I know because I'm the one who did the vaporizing...
NO, AT THE MOMENT THE PROPERTY IS EMPTY.
UP UNTIL SIX WEEKS AGO, THOUGH, IT WAS BEING LEASED TO A COMPANY CALLED RIDGE-FERRICK HOLDING HERE IN GOTHAM.

...and I did the vaporizing with a gun I found in the same warehouse.
SIX WEEKS.
TIMING'S RIGHT.
Charlie has a theory about both the gun and the thing.

THANKS FOR THIS, KATE.
NO, WAIT A MINUTE...

I don't like the theory, because it scares the crap out of me.
...WHAT'S THIS ABOUT? WHAT'S GOING ON?
I TOLD YOU, IT'S SOMETHING WE'RE LOOKING INTO.
Charlie's theory is that it's Intergang, that they're back, and that they're making a play for Gotham City...
YOU'RE NOT A P.I., RENEE. YOU'RE NOT LICENSED, I CHECKED!
AND WHOEVER YOUR "PARTNER" HERE IS, I DON'T THINK HE'S ONE EITHER!
KATE...
...moving in soldiers and weapons in preparation for a takeover.
NO! IF THIS IS SOMETHING THAT CONCERNS MY FAMILY, I HAVE A RIGHT TO KNOW!
YOU DON'T COME BACK INTO MY LIFE AFTER TEN YEARS ASKING FOR FAVORS WITHOUT AN EXPLANATION, RENEE!
YOU OWE ME THAT MUCH!
NO, I DON'T, KATE...
If he's right, and Intergang discovers we're on to them, they'll kill us both.
Then they'll go after any loose ends they think we've left behind.
...I DON'T OWE YOU ANYTHING.
Loose ends like her.
It's better that she stays away, that she doesn't know.
HOW...
...HOW CAN YOU SAY THAT...?
GOODBYE, KATE.

The meeting with Kate gets me two things. It gets me a lead, obviously...
...NO, REALLY, THAT WAS SMOOTH. NO WONDER THE WOMEN ARE FALLING ALL OVER THEMSELVES FOR YOU.
HEY, I GOT AN IDEA, WHY DON'T WE DOUBLE DATE SOMETIME!
...and it gives Charlie something else to bitch about besides my smoking.
WHAT WAS I SUPPOSED TO DO, HUH?
BAD ENOUGH WHAT INTERGANG WILL DO TO US THEY FIND OUT WE'RE MESSING WITH THEIR PLAY...
...MAYBE THEY LET US OFF WITH BEING LIGHTLY MURDERED, THAT'S FINE, THAT'S MY RISK, I'M WILLING TO TAKE IT.
BUT I SURE AS HELL AM NOT PUTTING KATE IN THEIR CROSSHAIRS AS WELL!
AHH, RIGHT...
...I SHOULD HAVE SEEN THAT, MY BAD.
WHAT? SHOULD HAVE SEEN WHAT?
THAT YOU STILL HAVE A THING FOR HER.
THE THING I HAD FOR HER ENDED TEN YEARS AGO, AND SHE ENDED IT.
I'M JUST TIRED OF PEOPLE I CARE ABOUT DYING ON ME, OKAY? BETTER SHE STAYS AWAY.
YOU'RE PACKING A LOT OF GUILT FOR SOMEONE SO YOUNG.
CHRP-CHRP-CHRP
AT LEAST I COME BY IT HONESTLY.
GIVE ME A BREAK.
WHAT DID YOU SAY?

WHAT DID YOU JUST--
YOU HEARD ME. THE THING WITH YOUR PARTNER, YOU'VE GOT TO LET THAT GO.
IT'LL EAT YOU ALIVE. TRUST ME, I'VE SEEN IT BEFORE.
OHIO 2004
BIG TOBACCO
HUB CITY
GOTHAM P.D.
CHECKMATE
YOU DON'T KNOW ANYTHING ABOUT--
MONTOYA
DETECTIVE SECOND GRADE CRISPUS ALLEN, MURDERED LAST WINTER.
CORRIGAN, JAMES, ARRESTED FOR THE KILLING, BUT RELEASED DUE TO LACK OF EVIDENCE. CASE IS STILL OPEN.
LUTHOR 986
JAMES CORRIGAN MURDERED YOUR PARTNER AND THEN WALKED.
ALLEN WAS YOUR PARTNER, AND HE WAS YOUR FRIEND, AND IT HAD TO BE ANSWERED. YOU OWED HIM THAT MUCH.
SO YOU HUNTED DOWN CORRIGAN AND YOU WANTED TO KILL HIM.
AND YOU DIDN'T DO IT.
AND THAT'S WHY YOU HATE YOURSELF, RENEE MONTOYA...
...BECAUSE YOU DID THE RIGHT THING.

GOT IT!
RIDGE-FERRICK HOLDING IS A SUBSIDIARY OF HSC INTERNATIONAL BANKING.
HSC INTERNATIONAL IS INTERGANG'S SPEARHEAD, ONE OF THEIR LEGIT FRONTS THEY ESTABLISH TO MOVE INTO NEW TERRITORY.
PART R&D, PART HUMAN RESOURCES.
THEY HAVE R&D?
THEY HAVE 401Ks, RENEE. THIS IS THE NEW INTERGANG, THEY'RE JUST AS HAPPY TO KILL YOU IN THE BOARDROOM AS IN THE BACK ALLEY.
HSC IS RUN BY A FORMER AGENT OF THE LATE RA'S AL GHUL.
THIS WOMAN, HERE, NAME OF WHISPER A'DAIRE, AND YES, IT'S OBVIOUSLY AN ALIAS.
A'DAIRE TRAVELS WITH A BODYGUARD-SLASH-LEGMAN...
...NAMED ABBOT. IF THAT'S HIS FIRST OR LAST I DON'T KNOW, BUT THE GUY'S A STONE-COLD KILLER.
IF THEY'RE HERE, THEN THERE'S NO QUESTION THAT INTERGANG HAS GOTHAM IN ITS SIGHTS.
SO WE NEED TO CONFIRM THAT THEY'RE HERE. WE NEED TO CONFIRM THEY'RE STILL MOVING IN PEOPLE AND EQUIPMENT.
EXACTLY.
AND HOW DO YOU SUGGEST WE DO THAT?
SAME WAY I GET MOST OF MY QUESTIONS ANSWERED...
PARK
...BREAKING AND ENTERING...

We've committed four misdemeanors and at least one felony just getting this far.
WILL YOU HURRY IT UP?
RIDGE-FERRICK
IF YOU CAN DO THIS FASTER, PLEASE BE MY GUEST.
It doesn't bother me.
HERE WE GO...
Charlie's influence, maybe...
...but I'm curious now, and I want some answers.
CAMERAS.
GOT IT.
And I have to admit it...
...there's a piece of me that's enjoying this...
QUIETLY.
...poking my nose where it clearly doesn't belong...
...asking the questions nobody else seems willing to ask.
...FOR THE SECOND STAGE, AS SCHEDULED.
ARMING THEM WON'T BE THE PROBLEM, BUT CONVERTING THE ACTUAL MANPOWER BASE.
WE'RE EXPECTING ANOTHER SHIPMENT FROM KAHNDAQ WITHIN THE MONTH.
Kahndaq... if Black Adam is part of this...
...
—there is no way this isn't about to suck.

It hits us like a large, furry brick...
GGRRRR
...hot breath blasts into my face, stinking of meat and blood...
NFFF
HNHH

...I try not to gag, try to get my gun...
GGRRRR

...and for a moment can't do anything but stare...
THAT'S ENOUGH...

...the wolf vanishes, but the stink remains, and then there's the sound of her voice...
LET'S HAVE A LOOK AT THEM, SHALL WE?
...the sound of something ancient sliding across scalding sands.

It's not her voice, though, it's her eyes...
AH, OUR FACELESS FRIEND, WHAT A SURPRISE...

...they lock on mine...
...BUT YOU, YOU'RE NEW...

...I can't look away...
...WHAT'S YOUR NAME, MORSEL?
RENEE MONTOYA.
...and I answer before I can stop myself.
Her tongue...
RENEE MONTOYA.
...Okay, that's gross.
...NICE TO HAVE MET YOU, HOWEVER BRIEFLY. MISTER ABBOT?
WHISPER?
THEY'LL HAVE TO DIE, I'M AFRAID.
WAIT WAITWAITWAIT WAIT...
...C'MON, DON'T YOU EVEN WANT TO KNOW WHY WE'RE HERE? WHAT WE HEARD?
THAT YOU HEARD ANYTHING IS ENOUGH TO SATISFY MY CURIOSITY, SIR.
GENTLEMEN, PLEASE...
...INDULGE YOURSELVES...
There's a sound as they begin to transform, like live wood snapping apart...

HEY, YOU KNOW THAT GUN FROM LAST TIME?
NOW WOULD PROBABLY BE A GOOD TIME TO USE IT.
A few weeks ago, just one of these things nearly killed both of us.
Even with the gun, I'm thinking that this time there's gonna be no way out of this alive.
KSSH KSSH KSSH KSSH
Then the lights go out.
I knew it.
All the talk, all the rumors...
...he didn't leave, he's still here...

...Gotham City will *always* have *Batman* to protect it...

Or not.
That's *not* Batgirl.
That's...
...that's a...
...that's a Bat*woman.*
Hot damn.
RAWGH--

So busy staring at her I almost miss him.
I've got the shot.
And just like Batman, she doesn't let me take it.
NO!
It's a good hit...
...somewhere along the line, someone taught her how to throw a punch...
...someone taught her how to...
...I'll be damned.

POLICE ARE EN ROUTE.
I'D APPRECIATE IT IF YOU KEPT ME OUT OF IT.
I THINK SHE LIKES YOU.
SHUT.
UP.

Week 11, Night 7
Opal City
...AND IT LOOKS FOR ALL THE WORLD LIKE SOMEONE UP AND TORE THAT DOOR RIGHT OFF ITS HINGES.
CALLED YOU RIGHT AWAY SO'S YOU COULD SEE WHAT ALL'S MISSING.
SORRY ABOUT THE DARK. WHOEVER BROKE IN SMASHED UP THE LIGHTS.
BEFORE OR AFTER THEY SIGNED THE DOOR?
RHETORICAL QUESTION. IGNORE IT.
THAT'S NOT THE MYSTERY HERE.
I HEARD ABOUT THIS "RESURRECTION CULT" ON THE RADIO...HELL, I'M SEEIN' THAT SYMBOL ON HALF THE HIGH SCHOOL KIDS IN MY NEIGHBORHOOD...BUT I FIGURED THEM FOR WACKOS, NOT THIEVES. WHAT'D THEY TAKE?

NOTHING IMMEDIATELY *EVIDENT*, BERNIE.
BUT *SOMETHING*, I'M SURE.

NEXT IN 52

WEEK ELEVEN NOTES

DAN DIDIO

I would be lying if I said I didn't think it was going to cause a stir. How big a stir, well, that caught me completely off guard. We knew we were going to put "new" characters into 52; that was always part of the plan, find a way to expand the way we see the DC Universe and the characters that inhabit it. We wanted to diversify our world to be more reflective of the real world and our readership. There is nothing unique about adding a lesbian character into the DCU. After all, this series had been featuring a lesbian, Renee Montoya, from the very first issue. What made Kate Kane unique is that she wore a bat symbol, so while the "real world" didn't know 52, it certainly knew Batman and she was one step removed.

It started with the *New York Times* (who used the phrase "Lipstick Lesbian," not me; someone had to explain to me what it meant) and snowballed from there. Newspapers, radio interviews and television news all found this to be worth reporting. And while you can argue its merits as news, there is no denying the response. Over a thousand e-mails (split 50/50 loving and hating) and one death threat, seems like the character struck a chord with the public even before they saw a single comics page with her on it.

I said it then and I feel it is worth repeating now: Batwoman is a hero first, and being lesbian only helps to define who she is and how she arrives at the choices she makes. I am proud of her addition to our pantheon of characters and although you are only meeting her briefly in this issue, we expect great things from her character in the future.

GREG RUCKA

The Charlie-and-Renee show really hit its stride in this issue, and that's just one of the many things that made this week so much fun to write.

Obviously, though, that's not the highlight here; the highlight is the return of Kate Kane and the big reveal — as opposed to the "weak" reveal on the 4th of July — of Batwoman. The art this issue rose to the task, as well; there's a panel on the fourth page where the acting between Montoya and Kate is beautifully subtle, each of them pretending to a nonchalance regarding the other that so clearly doesn't exist.

Charlie's line, "...no, really, that was smooth. No wonder the women are falling all over themselves for you. Hey, I got an idea, why don't we double date sometime!" was not the line as originally written. Originally, the line had Charlie saying, "...no, really [...] why didn't you just tell her you'd faked all your orgasms while you were at it?"

Some battles you just know you're going to lose, so you don't even bother to fight them, y'know? Still...it's the funnier line, you've got to admit.

The Batwoman reveal was one of those things that we all tried to pace out very carefully. I knew, in scripting it, that it would have to be a splash, just as I knew that Renee's internal monologue would have to be one that mistook Batwoman for Batman, at least at first. Normally I detest writing splash pages; I think they're a waste of precious real estate, and I think they've been overused to such an extent that they've lost all dramatic impact. This was one of the very rare cases where it was a no-brainer. There had to be the splash.

Alex Ross's proposed sketch was originally intended for a new "Batgirl" — but was repurposed later for Batwoman

For the most part, I don't mind not being a cop anymore.
G'NIGHT, CAPTAIN SAWYER.
GOOD NIGHT, REED.
POLICE
Week 12, Day 1
Gotham City.
I get to keep my own hours, I get to go where I want, and I don't have to deal with paperwork.

But there are downsides, and one of them is resources. You lose the badge, you lose that, too.
WHAT DO YOU WANT, RENEE?
The GCPD has over thirty thousand cops on the payroll.

HEARD THERE WAS A LITTLE TROUBLE AT RIDGE-FERRICK HOLDING LAST WEEK.
THAT WAS YOU?

You can't beat that for sheer manpower.
HOW MUCH DO YOU KNOW?
I KNOW THAT INTERGANG'S MAKING A MOVE ON GOTHAM, MAGGIE. RIDGE-FERRICK WAS THE CONDUIT.

NOT ANYMORE. THEY'VE CLOSED IT DOWN.
NOTHING LEFT IN THAT OFFICE BUT STAPLES AND BROKEN GLASS.

SO NOW INTERGANG KNOWS WE'RE ON TO THEM, AND WE DON'T HAVE THE FIRST IDEA HOW TO STOP THEM.
AND IF THEY ARE AFTER GOTHAM, YOU CAN BE DAMN SURE THEY'LL BE BACK!

YOU GAVE UP YOUR BADGE, RENEE, NOBODY TOOK IT FROM YOU.
REMEMBER THAT THE NEXT TIME YOU DECIDE TO PLAY HERO.

The sky opens on me halfway home.
Insult to injury.

I find Charlie exactly where I left him...
HI, HONEY...

...doing his impersonation of Sherlock Holmes-meets-the-Dalai Lama.
...I'M HOME.
He's been like this for the last two days. He calls it "going inside".
He says I should try it.
I.G. 36
I.G. 76

Like taking a good look at myself is something I would actually want to do right now.
Like that would answer the question of who the hell I am, what I'm doing with my life.
MILK

Intergang. Wolfman. Snake Fatale...
...Batwoman...
...questions...
TNK

Thing is, Maggie's right.
No way Intergang's giving up. They'll be back, if they're not still here.
They're moving weapons and people into Gotham. The only real way to fight that is to cut it off at the source.

So what's the source for their weapons and their people when both are easy enough to come by?
Except their weapons turn people to smoke...

...and their people transform into rejects from the Late, Late show.
Charlie's got thousands of notes here on Intergang...

...and one location keeps coming up again and again.
The same one we heard Whisper A'Daire mention at Ferrick-Ridge.
NNGK
If it's not the source, it's the next link in the chain.

It's the only lead we have.
ANYTIME YOU WANT TO STATE THE OBVIOUS IS FINE BY ME, CHARLIE.
If we're going to see this through, we have to follow it.

And Charlie knows it, too.
A'Daire
ALL RIGHT, YOU WIN...

...WE'LL GO TO KAHNDAQ.
DC COMICS 52

Writers: Johns, Morrison, Rucka, Waid

Breakdowns: Giffen
Pencils: Barrows
Inks: Stull
Letters: Lanham
Colors: Baron

Cover: Jones & Sinclair

Asst. Editors: Jones & Richards
Editor: Wacker

Week 12

MIGHTY

<THANK YOU.>

<IT IS HIM... OUR LEADER... OUR SAVIOR...>

<...BLACK ADAM!>

<THEY WORSHIP YOU LIKE A GOD.>
<IS THAT WHY YOU DO THIS?>

<...PLEASE. I AM YOUR LEADER, NOT YOUR RULER.>

<I ONLY DO WHAT I CAN TO HELP.>

<I HAD NO IDEA THIS VILLAGE WAS IN SUCH NEED.>
<THAT'S BECAUSE YOU'VE SPENT YOUR *TIME* AND ***POWER*** FIGHTING AMERICAN HEROES AND ***EXECUTING*** AMERICAN VILLAINS.>

<AND GATHERING TOGETHER COUNTRIES LIKE CHESS PIECES TO CONSOLIDATE A POWER BASE THAT ONLY SERVES TO THREATEN YOUR PEOPLE AND THE REST OF THE WORLD.>
<AND YOU DENY THE *THREATS* OF MISPLACED POWER?>
<POWER DOESN'T HAVE TO CORRUPT.>
<LOOK AT WHAT YOU'VE DONE THESE LAST FEW DAYS.>

<YOU CHANGED THE COURSE OF THAT RIVER AND PROVIDED WATER FOR HUNDREDS OF PEOPLE.>
<YOU DISARMED FIELDS OF MINES ACROSS KAHNDAQ'S HIGHWAYS.>

<YOU'VE MADE THEIR LIVES BETTER.>
<ALL BECAUSE YOU SUGGESTED IT.>
<AND THAT IS ALL *I* CAN DO. BUT SOMEONE LIKE YOU, BLACK ADAM. YOU SEE NOW, YOU CAN HELP IN SO MANY WAYS BECAUSE OF WHAT *YOU* CAN DO.>
<WHY ACT OUT OF ANGER WHEN YOU CAN ACT IN HOPE?>

<FOR A VERY GOOD REASON.>

<BLACK ADAM. WE HAVE BEEN WAITING FOR YOUR RETURN.>

<THE IRANIAN, SUPER-SHAYKH, HAS CONTACTED US AGAIN. HE IS WAITING.>
<HE NEEDS YOUR ASSISTANCE IN DEALING WITH THE SUPER-GROUP DARK NEMESIS. THEY JUST ATTEMPTED ANOTHER STRIKE AGAINST THEIR NUCLEAR WEAPONS FACILITY.>
<AND THEY WERE STOPPED?>
<THEY FLED, YES. BUT SUPER-SHAYKH IS STILL IN PURSUIT.>
<LATER THEN.>

<DO NOT DISTURB US.>
<BUT-->
<--LATER.>

<WHAT IS THIS PLACE?>
<A FEW YEARS AFTER THE WIZARD BESTOWED ME WITH THESE POWERS, MY WIFE AND SONS WERE *MURDERED.*>
<THEY WERE KILLED BY AN ENEMY I SHOULD HAVE DESTROYED LONG BEFORE.>
<I DESTROYED THEIR TOMB IN A BATTLE WITH THE JUSTICE SOCIETY OF AMERICA. I WAS BLINDED BY RAGE. BY *LOSS.*>
<YOU HAVE TO UNDERSTAND, I EXECUTE SO NO ONE ELSE WILL FEEL THE EMPTINESS THAT I DO.
THAT YOU *SURELY* DO.>

<INTERGANG KILLED YOUR FAMILY WHEN THEY KIDNAPPED YOU, THEY SOLD YOUR YOUNGER BROTHER INTO *SLAVERY.*>
<WHERE IS *YOUR* ANGER, ADRIANNA?>
<I'M NOT ANGRY.>
<YOU HAVE TO FEEL SOME-THING.>

<I'M NOT SURE WHAT I FEEL.>
<MOSTLY ALONE.>

CHANG
<WHAT ARE YOU--?>
KKKKKKRACKK
<WHERE DOES IT GO? A SECRET TUNNEL UNDER THE PALACE.>
<IT WILL TAKE US FAR FROM THE PALACE.>
<AND FROM KAHNDAQ.>
BILLY?
BLACK ADAM.

...AND NOW THE SEVEN SINS AND THE POWER WITHIN THE ROCK ARE UNDER MY WATCH.

I SEE SHAZAM'S NAME NO LONGER IGNITES A TRANSFORMATION IN EITHER OF US.
IT WILL AGAIN ONCE YOU LEAVE THE ROCK. IT TOOK ME TIME TO ADJUST TO SHAZAM'S POWER.
HAVE YOU COME TO TEAR ME IN HALF TOO?
OF COURSE, NOT. I'M NOT HERE TO FIGHT. I'M NOT YOUR ENEMY ANY-MORE, BILLY.

WELL, I SUPPOSE BEATING EACH OTHER UP NEVER REALLY SOLVED OUR PROBLEMS ANYWAY...

YOU SHOULDN'T HAVE COME HERE.
MR. ATOM. SABBAC. JOHNNY SORROW.
EVERY ADVERSARY I'VE HAD HAS ATTEMPTED A SIEGE UPON THE ROCK OF ETERNITY.
BUT WHAT NO ONE REALIZES IS THAT WITH THE WIZARD GONE, MY POWER WITHIN THE ROCK OF ETERNITY IS A HUNDRED-FOLD!
SHAZAM LEFT *ME* IN CHARGE, ADAM...

...WHO'S YOUR FRIEND?

MY NAME IS ADRIANNA TOMAZ.

QUIET!

THESE ARE MY GUESTS AND...
...YOU SHUT UP NOW. THAT'S RUDE, LUST!
AND YOU BETTER WATCH YOUR MANNERS TOO, ENVY. I'VE ALREADY CRUSHED GREED'S FACE, AND IT'LL TAKE FOREVER TO GROW BACK.
DON'T THINK I WON'T DO IT TO YOU, TOO!

SITTING ON THIS THRONE, YOU HEAR THE SINS CHATTER. AND THEY'RE AWFULLY MEAN.
ANYWAY, I'M VERY PLEASED TO MEET YOU, ADRIANNA.
WHAT BRINGS YOU BOTH HERE TO THE ROCK OF ETERNITY?

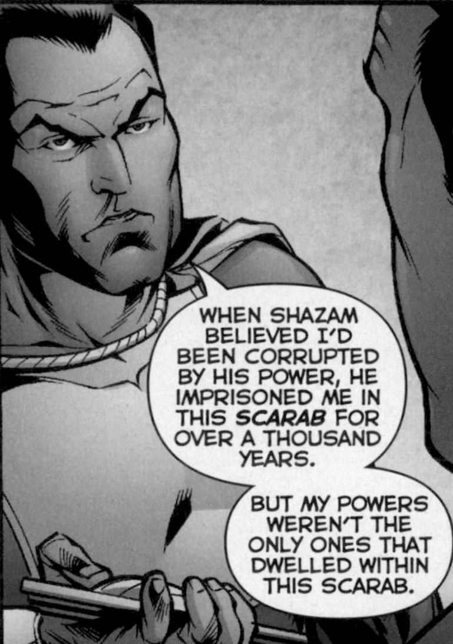
WHEN SHAZAM BELIEVED I'D BEEN CORRUPTED BY HIS POWER, HE IMPRISONED ME IN THIS SCARAB FOR OVER A THOUSAND YEARS.
BUT MY POWERS WEREN'T THE ONLY ONES THAT DWELLED WITHIN THIS SCARAB.

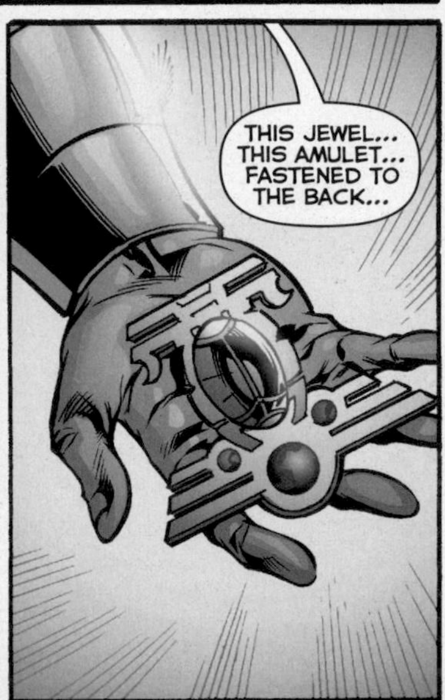
THIS JEWEL... THIS AMULET... FASTENED TO THE BACK...

...IT CONTAINED THE POWER OF ANOTHER ONE OF SHAZAM'S CHAMPIONS FROM ANCIENT EGYPT.
I WANT TO GIVE THAT POWER TO ADRIANNA.

WHAT?

I WANT TO INVITE HER INTO THE MARVEL FAMILY.

NEW MESSAGE 154
Cassie WHERE R U?

NEW MESSAGE 155
Wonder Girl,
Titans NEED YOU!
PLEASE RESPOND!

Philadelphia.

GO AHEAD, CASSIE.
TAKE YOUR CALLS.

MR. DIBNY! HOW... HOW DID YOU...
WHAT? GET IN? IT'S A TENEMENT APARTMENT, "MS. DONNA PRINCE," NOT THE PENTAGON.
FIND YOU? THAT'S WHERE PEOPLE ALWAYS GOT ME CONFUSED WITH PLASTIC MAN. HE'S THE CLOWN.
ELONGATED MAN IS THE DETECTIVE.

YOUR GANG GOT SLOPPY WHEN THEY ROBBED MY WIFE'S PERSONAL EFFECTS.
BETWEEN THE DNA YOU LEFT ON THE PULPED LOCKS AND THE SATELLITE PHOTOGRAPHY TRACKING THE FLIGHT PATH OF A SUPERHUMAN ROUGHLY YOUR SIZE...
...WELL, YOU PERSONALLY WERE PRACTICALLY SCREAMING TO BE FOLLOWED.

I CAN DO A LOT MORE THAN FLY, MR. DIBNY.
IS THAT A THREAT, WONDER GIRL? WHAT ELSE CAN YOU DO TO ME?
YOU ALREADY CONNED ME INTO TRUSTING YOU WHEN I BEGAN INVESTIGATING THE CULT OF CONNER.
I BLINKED, AND YOU BECAME A FANATIC ON THE RUN HIDING BEHIND A STRING OF-- FORGIVE ME-- PRETTY OBVIOUS ALIASES.

I CATALOGUED THE STORAGE LOCKER. ALL YOU AND YOUR GROUP STOLE WAS ONE OF SUE'S OUTFITS.
LET ME REPEAT THAT: YOU DID THOUSANDS OF DOLLARS' WORTH OF DAMAGE AND IGNORED TENS OF THOUSANDS WORTH OF JEWELRY TO TAKE A BLOUSE AND A SKIRT.
WHY?

YOU SAID IT YOURSELF WHEN YOU FIRST CAME TO ME, MR. DIBNY.
IN THIS ORIENTATION, THIS IS THE KRYPTONIAN SYMBOL OF RESURRECTION.
THE CULT OF CONNER BELIEVES IN SUPERBOY'S HOLY SPIRIT AND THAT HE WILL RETURN TO US SOMEDAY.

THIS IS FROM THE LIPS OF YOUR LEADER, DEVEM.
WE'RE ALL BELIEVERS, MR. DIBNY. BUT DEVEM'S TAKING US ONE STEP BEYOND FAITH.
HE SWEARS HE'S FOUND A METHOD IN THE HOLY TEXTS BY WHICH TO RAISE THE DEAD.

YOU HAVE TO BE--
--BUT IT'S A PROCESS WHICH REQUIRES... CONNECTIVE OBJECTS. THINGS THAT HAVE BEEN IN CLOSE CONTACT WITH THE DECEASED. HAIR... LOCKETS...
...CLOTHING...

OH, MY GOD.
CASSIE, THIS IS CRA--
YOU'RE AHEAD OF ME.

BEFORE TRYING TO REVIVE SUPERBOY, DEVEM WANTED TO MAKE A... TRIAL ATTEMPT.
BUT...

...BUT WHY SUE?
BECAUSE WE HAD SOMETHING FAR MORE PERSONAL AND INTIMATE THAN JUST A WARDROBE.
WE HAD A TALISMAN, A TOKEN SYMBOLIZING A LOVE STRONG ENOUGH TO REACH THE AFTERLIFE.

WE HAD YOUR WEDDING RING.
SO THAT'S IT. I'M SORRY, MR. DIBNY.
I'M SORRY I TRICKED YOU... BUT WE NEEDED WHAT YOU COULD GIVE, AND I KNEW YOU'D NEVER SUBMIT TO THIS WILLINGLY.

THEN YOU WERE WRONG.
WHAT?
YOU WERE WRONG.
YOU WANT TO RESURRECT MY WIFE FROM THE DEAD, CASSIE?

LET ME HELP.

<THE MAGICKS WITHIN THIS AMULET WERE GATHERED BY EGYPT'S MOST POWERFUL GODDESS--
--ISIS.>

<DURING THE 15TH DYNASTY, THE QUEEN, PHARAOH HATSHEPSUT, WAS GIFTED WITH THIS GREAT POWER.
HATSHEPSUT BROUGHT PEACE THROUGHOUT HER KINGDOM.>
<AFTER HER DEATH, THE POWERS RETURNED TO THIS AMULET-->
<--WHERE THEY STILL ARE. WAITING FOR HER NEXT CHAMPION-->
<--YOU, ADRIANNA.>

<THE SINS SEE FEW FLAWS IN HER.
AND SOLOMON TELLS ME SHE HAS HAD A PROFOUND EFFECT ON YOU THAT WILL ONLY GROW... SHE IS WORTHY.>
<SHE HAS ONLY TO TAKE THE AMULET AND-->

<STOP!>

<YOU WANT TO MAKE ME...
...YOU WANT TO MAKE ME LIKE YOU?>

<YOU'LL BE MORE POWERFUL THAN I, ADRIANNA. YOU'LL BE A GODDESS.>
<I'M NOT A GODDESS. I'M JUST A WOMAN.
THAT'S ALL I WANT TO BE.>

<THINK OF WHAT YOU WILL BE ABLE TO DO. FOR THE PEOPLE. AND FOR YOURSELF.>
<NOTHING WILL BE ABLE TO STOP YOU. YOU'LL NEVER BE HURT BY ANYTHING OR ANYONE AGAIN.>
<BUT... P-POWER CORRUPTS.>
<IT NEED NOT. YOU SAID THAT YOURSELF.>
<YOU'VE ONLY JUST BEGUN TO SHOW ME A NEW WAY.>
<I NEED YOUR HELP. I NEED SOMEONE AT MY SIDE.>
<TAKE THE AMULET, ADRIANNA.
LET THE WORDS FLOW INTO YOU...>
<...AND THROUGH YOU.>
<I HEAR IT. A SIMPLE PRAYER.>
<SAY IT, ADRIANNA.>
<SAY IT.

I AM ISIS!

<ADRIANNA?>
<NO, TETH ADAM.>

<CALL ME BY MY NEW NAME.>

<STOP SNORING, SLOTH!>
<AND YOU CAN STOP BRAGGING, PRIDE. THIS WHOLE AFFAIR HAS NOTHING TO DO WITH YOU!>

<I FEEL HER POWER INSIDE OF ME, ADAM.>
<NATURE IS CALLING ME. ASKING ME WHAT IT CAN DO TO HELP MY CRUSADE.>

<I'M HOPING IT WILL BE OUR CRUSADE.>
<HELP ME, ISIS.>

<HELP ME CHANGE THE WORLD FOR THE BETTER.>
<I WILL, ADAM.>
<I WILL JOIN YOU ON YOUR MISSION...>

<...AS SOON AS WE FIND MY BROTHER.>
NEXT IN

WEEK TWELVE NOTES

J.G. JONES

Week 12 proved to be one of the most difficult covers for me to do. I think I counted over 30 sketches that I did for this issue before we went with the existing image of Black Adam and Isis flying together in a loving embrace.

It was not a problem of deciding who to cast on the cover. This issue's big moment is the creation of Isis, Black Adam's new love. I wanted to show the two of them together on the cover in a setting that suggested the Kingdom of Kahndaq. I also knew that I wanted to show the two of them exhibiting affection towards one another.

No, the problem was how to present the moment. I probably was overthinking the whole thing, but I put so much pressure on myself to come up with just the right moment that I think I froze up and could not make any decision. The sketches kept getting more and more complicated, with more and more elements being added.

I had to finally step back and reassess the whole thing. I had to pare it back to the essentials. I took note of the fact that Isis wears white, while Black Adam wears...well, black. Then it occurred to me that Isis brings out the best in Adam, which made me think of the yin-yang symbol, with black and white intertwined.

I think it was Steve Wacker's idea to have Adam carrying the flag of Kahndaq to show that he represents his nation. Finally, I painted in the giant Egyptian-style stone head in the background to give a sense of location, and the whole thing fell into place.

I asked Alex Sinclair to keep the color simple on this cover. I wanted to emphasize the duality of the black and white. Both wear gold, a symbol of purity, so the third color was gold and variations on gold (the sandy-colored background).

I learned a lot from the process of creating this cover that followed me in creating the rest of the 52 covers. Sometimes simple is best.

PENCILS

The original pencilled page by **Eddy Barrows** featuring the debut of Isis!

WRITTEN BY GEOFF JOHNS, GRANT MORRISON, GREG RUCKA, MARK WAID
BREAKDOWNS BY KEITH GIFFEN

FOR RAO, FIRE IS THE HEAT OF LIFE...
TRANSMITTING...
GREEN LANTERN, CAN YOU *HEAR* ME?
LIKE YOU'RE *UNDERWATER*, RALPH. I'VE NEVER USED THE RING TO MAKE TELEPATHIC PLUGS BEFORE, AND THEY'RE A BITCH...BUT WE'RE CONNECTED.
ARROW?

PE CILS BY TODD NAUCK • INKS BY MARLO ALQUIZA • COLORS BY ALEX SINCLAIR

LETTERING BY NICK J. NAPOLITANO • COVER BY J.G. JONES & ALEX SINCLAIR

ASSISTANT EDITORS JANN JONES & HARVEY RICHARDS

EDITED BY STEPHEN WACKER

THEY WANT TO RESURRECT MY WIFE.

Week 13

HAYSTACK

LOOK AROUND YOU. THAT'S CRAZY TALK.
IS IT, OLLIE? REALLY?
IN YOUR NAME, RAO--
A FEW YEARS AGO, AS I RECALL, YOU WENT UP IN A FIERY BLAST TO STOP SOME TERRORISTS.

YOU WERE D-E-A-D.
--WE SLAKE OUR THIRST WITH THE WATERS OF MEMON!
NOW YOU'RE BACK.

ZAURIEL, WE ALL ACCEPT THAT YOU REPRESENT HEAVEN ITSELF! YOUR AFTERLIFE HAS A REVOLVING DOOR.
HAL, YOU DIED AND WERE GIVEN MISSIONS BY GOD HIMSELF BEFORE YOU WERE SENT SHUFFLING BACK TO THIS MORTAL COIL.

IN YOUR NAME, RAO--WE WARM OUR BONES BY THE FIRES OF THRENTAR!

AND REX, NOT TO PUT TOO FINE A POINT ON IT, BUT I'VE HONESTLY LOST TRACK OF THE NUMBER OF TIMES YOU'VE BEEN D.O.A.

THAT'S WHY I CALLED ON YOU FOUR SPECIFICALLY.
I'M HOPING AT LEAST ONE OF YOU CAN SPEAK TO WHAT'S HAPPENING HERE...
AND IN YOUR NAME, RAO--

...BECAUSE THERE IS ABSOLUTELY NO EVIDENCE THAT WHAT'S BEING PREACHED HERE TODAY IS ANY CRAZIER THAN YOUR STORIES.
--WE SURRENDER OURSELVES TO THE REMNANTS OF YOUR LAND!

BLOOD KRYPTONITE. PASS IT FROM HAND TO HAND AMONG YOU.
LET IT DRAW FROM EACH OF US A SMALL FRACTION OF OUR LIFE ESSENCE--

--SO THAT IT MAY IN TURN CREATE THE DIVINE ENERGY NECESSARY TO MAKE FLESH THE FORM BEFORE US!

RALPH, TELL US THIS IS A RUSE.
WHAT HAPPENED TO SUSAN WAS TRULY *TRAGIC*... BUT DON'T LET THAT PAIN *DELUDE* YOU.

--*NOR*--AND I REALIZE HOW HYPOCRITICAL THIS MIGHT SOUND--DOES IT SOUND LIKE A SANE *IDEA*.
AT ALL.
RALPH, I'VE KNOWN YOU FOR *YEARS*.

IN FACT, I'M THE ONE WHO ORIGINALLY ASKED THE ELONGATED MAN TO *JOIN* THE JUSTICE LEAGUE, REMEMBER?
REX...OLLIE... WE'VE ALL FOUGHT *GODS* ALONGSIDE YOU. THERE IS *NOTHING* WE WOULDN'T DO IN THE NAME OF THAT *FRIENDSHIP*.

SO DO YOU HONESTLY THINK THAT IF *ANY* OF US HAD *ANY POWER WHATSOEVER* TO BRING SUE BACK TO YOU, WE WOULDN'T HAVE DONE IT THE *DAY SHE DIED?*
FOR GOD'S SAKE, YOU DIDN'T ASK US HERE TO *VALIDATE* A *CEREMONY*.

"BLOOD KRYPTONITE." FROM WHERE? IT'S A *PAINTED ROCK*, RALPH. A *SPECIAL EFFECT* DESIGNED TO PREY ON *SUGGESTIBLE CHILDREN*.
HE'S ON TO SOMTHIN'. THE FIRES ARE A *CHEMICAL SHOW*. I CAN TELL. THE WATER-FALL? *COLORED LIGHTS*.

YOU WANTED FRIENDS HERE TO GIVE YOU PERSPECTIVE BECAUSE, IN YOUR HEART OF HEARTS, YOU'RE AFRAID YOU'VE COFUSED DESPERATION, FOR JUDGMENT.
AND YOU HAVE.
UNNHH...

OKAY, THAT TEARS IT. REAL OR FAKE, I'M CUTTING IN--!
NOT OUR DECISION, OLLIE. STOP.

RALPH... MORE THAN BRUCE, MORE THAN BARRY...
...YOU HAVE ALWAYS BEEN THE MOST RATIONAL MAN I KNOW.

BUT I ALSO KNOW HOW IMPORTANT IT IS TO BELIEVE.
WHAT HAPPENS NEXT IS UP TO YOU. WE WILL BACK OFF, OR WE WILL STEP IN.

EITHER WAY, IT'S YOUR CALL.

Southwest Asia.

<BLACK ADAM!>

<THIS SLAVERY RING ENDS NOW. AS DOES YOUR LIFE.>

<NO, ADAM. WE DON'T NEED TO KILL THEM.>
<LET THEM BE JUDGED FOR THEIR CRIMES IN THIS LIFE.>
<AND WHEN NATURE TAKES ITS COURSE, THE NEXT.>

<NOTHING WILL ESCAPE NATURE, ADAM. AND AS ISIS, I AM NATURE.>
<WINDS.>

THOOOMMMMM

<THEY DESERVE MORE THAN A FEW BROKEN BONES.>
<NO, ADAM.>

<NOT IN FRONT OF THE CHILDREN.>
<THANK YOU.>
<THANK YOU.>
<THANK YOU.>
<THANK YOU.>
<THANK YOU.>

<IT'S ALL RIGHT. YOU'RE ALL GOING HOME.>

<MOST OF THEM DON'T HAVE HOMES TO GO TO, ADRIANNA.>
<BEFORE I RETOOK KAHNDAQ, THE DICTATOR THERE DRAGGED THOUSANDS OF CHILDREN FROM THEIR HOMES, FORCING THEM INTO HARD LABOR AND PROSTITUTION.>
<THE PARENTS THAT ARGUED WERE KILLED ON SIGHT.>

<THEN... THEN THE ORPHANS OF THE WORLD ARE WELCOME IN KAHNDAQ.>
<ALL OF THEM...>

<...ALL OF THEM WE CAN FIND.>

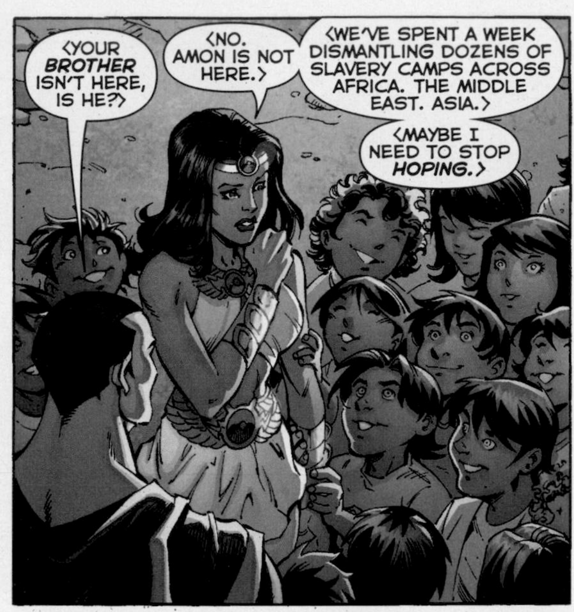
⟨YOUR BROTHER ISN'T HERE, IS HE?⟩
⟨NO. AMON IS NOT HERE.⟩
⟨WE'VE SPENT A WEEK DISMANTLING DOZENS OF SLAVERY CAMPS ACROSS AFRICA. THE MIDDLE EAST. ASIA.⟩
⟨MAYBE I NEED TO STOP HOPING.⟩

⟨STOP HOPING?⟩
⟨LOOK AT THESE CHILDREN, ADRIANNA.⟩

⟨THAT'S ALL THEY ARE DOING NOW.⟩
⟨YOU SHOW THEM HOPE.⟩

⟨YOU SHOW ME HOPE.⟩
⟨AND NO ONE HAS DONE THAT IN SO LONG...IN SO MANY CENTURIES...⟩

⟨WE WILL FIND YOUR BROTHER.⟩

⟨AND WE'LL FREE ALL THE CHILDREN IN THE WORLD DOING IT.⟩

HEY, REX?

YEAH, RALPH?

REMEMBER HOW WE DEALT WITH *KANJAR RO'S* GAMMA GONG THAT TIME?

LIKE IT WAS *YESTERDAY.*
WELCOME *BACK,* PAL.
KRUMP
YOU *HEARD* THE MAN! LET'S *GO,* PEOPLE!

NO! WHAT ARE YOU DOING?
SHUTTING DOWN AN ENORMOUS CON, YOU PARASITE!
I'M NOT SURE WHAT YOU HOPED TO GAIN BY STRINGING ME ALONG, BUT YOU PICKED THE WRONG VICTIM!

WHO CONNED WHO, DIBNY?
WONDER GIRL!

YOU PLAYED ME TO GET IN! THIS IS A SACRED CEREMONY!
HOW DARE YOU RUIN THIS FOR US?

I LOVED SUPERBOY! I WANT HIM BACK!
IF YOU COST ME THAT--!
WAKE UP, CASSIE! YOU'VE BEEN BRAINWASHED BY-- NNNGH!

YOU DON'T KNOW THAT!
YOU DON'T KNOW ANY-THING!

SHE THINKS SHE CAN SNARE YOU WITH A YELLOW ROPE?
SHE DIDN'T GET THE MEMO. NEW RULES.
IT'S CASSIE, RIGHT? CASSIE, CALM DOWN. WE'RE ONLY HERE TO HELP.

YEAH, THIS IS GOIN' WELL.
YOU'D BE SURPRISED HOW OFTEN THIS HAPPENS WHEN SOMEONE LETS ME INTO A CHURCH.
EVERYBODY FUNNEL THESE KIDS OUTSIDE BEFORE SOMEONE GETS TRAMPLED!

THIS WAY! HURRY!

WHAT ABOUT WONDER GIRL?
LEAVE HER! SHE SHOULD HAVE KNOWN BETTER!

THAN WHAT? TO TRUST A SCAM ARTIST WITH A SICK MIND?
WHOK

DIBNY, YOU DON'T UNDERSTAND--!

SHUT YOUR MOUTH, YOU PIECE OF FILTH!
YOU TWISTED ME AND YOU MANIPULATED ME AND YOU PUT ME THROUGH HELL!

AND FOR WHAT?

RALPH...?
YOU IDIOT.
OH, GOD... OH, GOD, WHAT HAVE I...?
STOP! STOP!
RALPH, WHAT--?

HNNNNH!
NEVER MIND! JUST GET OUT OF HERE! GO!
NO! I WAS WRONG! WE WERE WRONG!
HAL, THIS WASN'T A TRICK!

PLEASE! I--I SHOULD HAVE BELIEVED! WE HAVE TO TRY AGAIN--!
HOW? WE HAVE NO SACRED WATERS! WE HAVE NO KRYPTONITE! THANKS TO YOU--

--WE HAVE NOTHING!
WAIIIIIT!

HOW MANY ARE LEFT INSIDE?
MORE THAN I WAS PREPARED TO *EVACUATE!*
HANG ON, RALPH! WE'RE COMING!

JUST **HANG** ON!

KRSSSH

Week 13, Day 3
NO REMAINS.
THAT'S THE GOOD NEWS, RIGHT?

IN THAT THE RING DIDN'T FIND HIS BODY, YES. RALPH MAY NO LONGER BE USING HIS ELASTIC POWERS, BUT HE EVIDENTLY STILL GOT OUT ALIVE.

AND WENT WHERE?
THAT'S THE BAD.

THERE'S NOT A TRACE OF HIM, DAMN IT.
NOT A ONE.

POOR RALPH. EVEN AFTER HE THOUGHT HE'D LOST EVERYTHING, HE STILL HAD HIS MIND. NOW...

...NOW WHAT HAPPENS...?
SYDCO

TRY AGAIN...TRY AGAIN...

TO BE CONTINUED IN 52 VOLUME TWO

WEEK THIRTEEN NOTES

MARK WAID

Editor Steve Wacker promised me first crack at our spinoff series, ALL-STRAW SUE DIBNY. Then he left the company and took with him my dreams.

Now that I've gassed on and on about what a collaborative creative effort each 52 script was, let's discuss the flip side to that. Yes, we worked in close concert and, yes, we co-plotted the major storylines...but, particularly as we all began to get more comfortable with the writing process, we came away less and less often from every plot-conference call having hammered down every last little rivet. There were two reasons for this, both related to maintaining some sense of personal pride despite our mutual devotion to the Great Hivemind.

First, everyone wants to feel like they're carrying their weight by bringing new ideas to the table. This is particularly important when you're working alongside Grantiac, who generates more new ideas in the time it takes to sneeze than most of us will have in a year.

Second, fun and energetic conference calls full of mutual ego-boosting are what got the writers through the days, but the thrill of surprise is what got us through the lonely nights. If all your plot beats are too stringently mapped before you sit down to write, the job is no fun and quickly degenerates from creating into simply typing.

All this is to say that while I cannot lay claim to the idea of building a religious cult around the late Kon-El — that may have been Geoff, since Kon was his favorite character — I do remember hiding Wicker Sue from my collaborators for as long as possible, gambling that when they met her cold on the page, they'd be as revulsed and disturbed by her as I was. (And, no, I haven't the slightest idea what dark corner of my psyche she sprang from, but the point is, as writers who make our living using shock and surprise as tools, it's only natural that we'd enjoy startling each other sometimes. We're all a little bit competitive. And when Keith — who is the scariest, creepiest, most menacing life form I know — called me to tell me how much Wicker Sue made his skin crawl, that was a very good day.)

Enough about The Wonder of Me. Some other notes:

In the script, Zauriel was Hawkwoman. I was going for the reincarnation angle, completely forgetting that as last seen in Week Five, she was still twenty feet tall. Good catch, Wacker.

Astute readers will notice a figure lurking in the background of page twenty. I thought I knew who it was when I put him there, but as we'll see come week 42, I was mistaken. Also, Ralph's uncanny resemblance in this shot to cover artist J.G. Jones is purely coincidental (I pray).

BREAKDOWNS

BY **KEITH GIFFEN**

Artist Keith Giffen had the monumental task of laying out a full issue of breakdowns per week. To keep up the level of fun during the chaotic schedule of 52, he would often create "gag" pages such as this one.

THE **PROCESS**

Breaking down the final page of **week 13**

Original Script

PANEL ONE:

Ralph — singed, weeping, rocking back and forth — sits in the homeless-land filth under the overpass, cradling all that's left of wicker Sue – a charred, armless and legless torso and most of a head.

RALPH: ...try AGAIN...

PANEL TWO:

Pull back to see that he's being observed by a mystery figure who will, at least according to our plans, be later revealed as ~~Felix Faust.~~

Breakdown by Keith Giffen

Pencils by Todd Nauck

Final Page

COVER GALLERY

ART BY **J.G. JONES** WITH **ALEX SINCLAIR**

WEEK **ONE**

WEEK **TWO**

WEEK **THREE**

WEEK **FOUR**

WEEK **FIVE**

WEEK **SIX**

WEEK **SEVEN**

WEEK **EIGHT**

WEEK **NINE**

WEEK **TEN**

WEEK **ELEVEN**

WEEK **TWELVE**

WEEK **THIRTEEN**